THE
COURAGE OF
TURTLES

THE COURAGE
OF TURTLES

Fifteen essays about compassion, pain, and love, about being
at home, about rodeos, the circus, and boxing, about being a WASP,
about county fairs and radicalism and taxidermy, about being
a writer, about tugboats, bear-hunting, the courage of the
animal kingdom . . . and other sundries of Americana

EDWARD HOAGLAND

LYONS & BURFORD, PUBLISHERS

Printed in the United States of America

10 9 8 7 6 5 4 3 2 1

Library of Congress Cataloging-in-Publication Data

Hoagland, Edward
    The courage of turtles: fifteen essays about compassion, pain, and love.../Edward Hoagland.
            p.   cm.
    Originally published: New York: Random House [1970].
With new introd.
    ISBN 1-55821-215-9
    I. Title.
PS3558.0334C68 1993
814'.54—dc20   92-38600
                                                    CIP

FOR M., AGAIN
AND FOR MOLLY

CONTENTS

Publisher's Note

We're proud to be bringing Edward Hoagland's two distinguished collections of essays, *The Courage of Turtles* and *Walking the Dead Diamond River*, back into print. We thought a brief introduction might help put them into context and the single one the author wrote applies to both books, so rather than choose one or the other, we've taken the unusual course of running it in both.

It's fun to see these two essay collections, *The Courage of Turtles* and *Walking the Dead Diamond River*, bounce back into print. They were written with a kind of gleeful fluidity twenty years ago when I was in my late thirties, which is an age when many writers hit their stride, and for me they constituted a second wind. Earlier I had published three novels, but was stalled on the fourth, and meanwhile had discovered essay-writing through the vehicle of a long travel journal, *Notes from the Century Before*, which I published in 1969, about the old men of Telegraph Creek, a frontier hamlet on the Stikine River in British Columbia about eight hundred miles north of Vancouver.

Wilds had intrigued me since my teens, when I had ridden horseback for a summer in Wyoming, then had fought forest fires in the Santa Ana Mountains in southern California another summer, and had joined the Ringling Bros. and Barnum & Bailey Circus for two spells of caring for the big cats. I'd written a novel about the latter experience; a second about New York boxing; and another one about a Pied Piper's adventures in a Manhattan welfare hotel. Fiction was my first love—I wanted to be the great American novelist—but I lacked the exceptional memory that novelists need. (Montaigne in his essay "On Liars" says he found "scarcely a trace of it" in himself: "I do not believe there is another man in the world so hideously lacking.") Perhaps as a result I had focused upon honing a poetic style, which is an inadequate substitute, though I spent an hour for every ten words that appeared in my novels.

Now, however, I wrote the thirty-four essays in these two books breezily abruptly in just four years, with a new baby enlivening the house besides, and published many of them in the *Village Voice*, whose offices were located a few blocks down the street from where I lived. My stuff thus came out immediately, and instead of reaching three or four thousand people, might be placed in the hands of one hundred and fifty thousand. On the Staten Island ferry or the Coney Island subway I could see it read, and was plumbing heartfelt material, not filtered through the artifices of fiction. Though paid only $35 for a piece such as "The Courage of Turtles"— which of course I'd tried at *The New Yorker*, the *Atlantic*, and what not—I wasn't writing primarily for money or even fame, but simply to speak. A bad stutter had rendered me functionally mute for years, and this at last was my breakthrough.

There are phases of life. As a young novelist I lived on the Lower East Side in New York or near Boston's skid row (was once kicked out of a rooming house for pissing in my sink in order not to have to climb the stairs), earning fifty cents an hour, yet I was indefatigably quick-footed and often high-hearted because I believed I might be Leo Tolstoy. All around, as early as college, I had watched my contemporaries trim their sails. But I hadn't; no ceiling had appeared overhead to crimp my hopes. I strode the streets hungering for experience, convinced that every mile I walked the better writer I'd be, and, after making love, rolled out of bed (while my friend patiently laughed) to crouch next to my pants and scribble in a pocket notebook thoughts coitus might have brought. Hassles with the landlord about heat in the winter I could take; what mattered was that I was *good*. Until eventually the worm of doubt, a decade out, spoiled this bohemian gaiety. But I married, had a child, bought a $5,000 country house with money my grandmother had left me, and stumbled on the discovery that my main bent was for essay-writing.

I won't try to describe the changes New York City has undergone in twenty years. Like mine, they'd need more space. In the country, I mourned in these books the loss of Vermont's moose, epitomized by the head mounted on a wall in the local bank ("The Moose on the Wall"). Yet what has happened is that moose instead of vanishing have since come back. One afternoon a curious bull moose stepped right onto my front lawn because my rooster was crowing. Culturally, the town I live in has become somewhat suburbanized. Both of the old taxidermy shops have closed, the raunchy girlie shows have been banished from the county fair, and a five-hundred-acre dairy farm has been converted to a nine-hole golf course where the middle class cavorts. Yet from higher up on Barton Mountain, the resurgent moose, black bears, and coyotes of a new subspecies, New England-variety, gaze down on the golfers. Coyotes now den every spring on the ridge a quarter-mile above my house, and bears have tried to den in my hayloft.

The bears' close presence in the fall has marked with a degree of reassurance the two bad sieges that I have suffered during the past ten years. I went nearly blind for a spell, and I'd been suicidal at an earlier point, not from the incipient blindness but trouble with my marriage. Blind one year and suicidal another, I lay on my lawn in cherry season listening to a family of bears pull the branches down and strip and munch the fruit and leaves. It may have been the same mother with different cubs, but in any case they seemed to know that under the present circumstances I was no threat to them and came within thirty yards of me, masticating steadily and muttering a high-and-low pitched nattering commentary to each other. I felt utterly calm. When blind, I knew that until my eyes were operated on the problem was that I lay dying, not that any bear bore me ill will. And when suicidal, I merely enjoyed their gourmand greediness, glad my apple trees and chokecherries would help them sleep plumply through the lengthy winter. I was not afraid of them, or auto accidents, plane crashes, walking pneumonia, falling off a mountainside, robbers, vandals. I was afraid because I'd gone that day to a friend's general store to price handguns. He had a lot—used to bootleg them to New York City—and for $79.99 he'd offered me a nickel-plated Colt .32-caliber six-shot revolver some seventy years old, plus cartridges enough to blow my brains out thirty times over. The gun had gone from hand to hand since Prohibition, but I didn't buy it. So the bears and I were enjoying this quiet evening as they prepared their physiology for the winter and as I loaded up on cousinhood and tranquility like a layer of fat and ballast for the months to come.

Summer auction prices in Vermont have gone sharply up in twenty years, while most of the forests that I walked through have been cut down. But the underlying tracts of land are still intact, sprouting moose food. I used to descend from one of the firetower mountains with my billygoat and dog (first a collie, then a husky), and, if I had been camping overnight, would stop for a big meal at a restaurant in Island Pond called the Buck and Doe, which was owned by the chef, who was a "black" man from Boston (he was actually brown); then go on with a jug of wine to a nearby commune where I had some friends (and where several of the women liked to hoe barebreasted in the garden because they thought that helped things grow). I'd share a twilight supper of greens with them, but head home alone as the LSD was broken out for various people's "trips" and be at work by dawn. I was faithful to my wife, who by choice usually stayed in the city, and she to me during these happy years. We had a marriage based on the principle that opposites attract and she kept my nature writing suitably skeptical; our friction for the first decade was a creative one. Later, when it wasn't and she went her separate way, I had two deep-dyed love affairs in Vermont: with a woman who made artwork of stained glass and with a sociology professor whose memory also lights these country roads for me at night. My essays grew a bit more cagey, nuanced, gloomy, finding for the second time that the world was not an oyster, after all.

The gandy dance of sex and courtship acquires over a lifetime a sort of continental scope. You look back and see that *this* three-hundred-mile stretch of track was accomplished with a Chinese-American's help; *this* with an Italian; a Jew; a Scandinavian. And similarly an oeuvre piles up book by book, flawed in the struggle but each done with good will; and, glancing back, one remembers passing through *these* mountains, *this* lovely canyon. No stretch of my career was more fun than the months from autumn 1968 to spring 1973, whose output is here.

—EDWARD HOAGLAND
Fall 1992

THE
COURAGE OF
TURTLES

THE PROBLEM

OF THE

GOLDEN RULE

Like a good many New Yorkers, I've often wondered whether I was going to be mugged. I've lived in a number of neighborhoods, and being a night walker, have many times changed my course or speeded my stride, eying a formidable-looking figure as he approached. But it's never happened, and I imagine that if it finally does there may actually be a kind of relief, even a species of exhilaration, as I pick myself up—assuming that I am not badly hurt—because a danger anticipated for a long time may come to seem worse than the reality. People who come home and encounter a robber in their apartment who flees are likely to be less shaken up than the householder is who simply steps into a shambles of ransacked bureaus and upended beds: they've seen the fellow; they know he's human. A friend of mine wrestled a burglar for several minutes around the floor of his living room, both of them using the trips and hip throws that they remembered from their teens, until by the time my friend won and phoned the police they were old acquaintances.

I know, too, that to describe the few incidents of violence I've met with in the past makes them sound more grisly than they were in fact. In the army, my platoon was put in the charge of a peculiar sergeant who, mostly for reasons of his own, had us do squat jumps one noontime until we could no longer walk or stand up. Then he strolled among us kicking us to make sure that we weren't faking. It was a hot drill field strewn with packs and stacked rifles and other movie props, and yet the experience was not nearly as bad as one would anticipate if he were told at breakfast what to expect that day. We just followed orders until we couldn't get up and then we lay where we were on the ground until the sergeant was satisfied that we had done what was humanly possible. Even in a true atrocity situation that's all that is ever done: what is humanly possible. Afterwards one becomes unresponsive and fatalistic; terror is no longer a factor.

Next day the sergeant wanted to have it both ways, so he set us into formation and told us what he was going to make us do, and thereupon went off to the latrine to give us a chance to stand at attention and think and stew. Another sergeant promptly walked up and dismissed us, however. We hobbled away in every direction as fast as possible, while the two sergeants met to discuss the issue in the barracks door. They met person-to-person, and we had been punished person-to-person, and the facelessness of the mugger whom one anticipates meeting on Little West 12th Street was never a part of it. This, like our doing

4

whatever was humanly possible, made the experience supportable.

I visualize Armageddon not as a steel-muzzled affair of push-button silos under the earth but as a rusty freighter, flying the Liberian flag, perhaps, which sails inconspicuously up the Hudson past my apartment and goes off. Beyond that I don't see any details—though, as a non sequitur, I expect the tunnels and bridges would fill up with hikers leaving the city before it was too late. A woman I know says she sees Armageddon as getting under the bed. What we do with the insupportable is to turn it to terms we can file and forget. Unfortunately we are able to deal almost as handily with the nuclear bombs that have already gone off as we are with the ones that haven't. If as individual fighting men we had razed Hiroshima, then the horror of its destruction would persist as a legend to our greatgrandchildren because it would have been witnessed and done on the spot—also because of the somber old notion that residing in every man is a spark of divinity, whether the man is an enemy or a friend. This putative spark is central to most religious belief; and right at the root of Western ethics is what is called, under one of its names, the Golden Rule. But spark or no spark, since in practice we cannot react to others with unabashed fellow-feeling, we usually reduce the Golden Rule to a sort of silver rule, doing to them just about what we think they would do to us if they had the opportunity. And this works—has been working—though the new impersonalized technology is challenging its workability, along with another behemoth among changes, which is that today there are too many people. Where there are too many people, we get tired of following even the silver rule, tired of paying that much attention, of noticing whom we are with and who is who. For the agnostic as well, basing his reverence for life on its variety and on a Jeffersonian fascination with the glimmerings of talent in every man, the glut is discouraging. Although we don't ridicule these old ideas, the sentiments that people have for one another in a traffic jam are becoming our sentiments more and more. A groan goes up in any suburb when it's announced that a new complex of housing for two thousand souls is going to be built on Lone Tree Hill. And the vast sigh of impatience which greeted Pope Paul's traditionalist statement of faith in the sanctity of the seed germs of life points to the tone to come. *Life for the living,* people will say: body-counts in war and baby-counts in peace. We grant each union man his $10,500 a year, and then the hell with him. He, for his part, doesn't care if our garbage cans fester with rats when the union goes after $10,900.

Never have people dealt so briskly with strangers as now. Many of us have ceased to see strangers at all; our eyes simply don't register them except as verticals on the sidewalk, and when we must parley with them we find out quickly what they are asking from us, do it—maybe— and that's that. When I was a child I remember how my astonishment evolved as I realized that people often would not do the smallest thing to convenience another person or make him feel easier for the moment. Of course I'd known that *kids* wouldn't, but I had thought that was because they were kids. It was my first comprehension of the deadness of life. Everyone has discovered at some particular point life's deadness, but the galloping sense of deadness which alarms so many people lately, and especially the young, goes way beyond such individual discoveries to dimensions and contexts that have brought revolution to the U.S. Even in the arts the ancient austerities have been deemed insufficient, and we have actors who jump into the audience and do their acting there. When acting seems to fail, they improvise, and finally improvisation isn't enough either, and instead of having an actor play the drug addict, the addict himself must appear onstage and play himself—like the toothpaste tube blown up and hanging on the museum wall: "Look, if nothing else, I'm real." This is the era when students are so busy trying to teach their teachers that they are hard to teach, and when the chip on the shoulder of the man in the street is his "personality"—personality is quarrelsomeness. The revolution, in any case, is overdue, but maybe our best hope is that we remain at least idiosyncratic creatures, absorbed close to home. Dog owners, when they walk their dogs, show nearly as exact an interest in their pets' defecations as they would in their own. The same communing silence steals over their faces, the look of musing solemnity, that usually only the bathroom mirror gets a glimpse of.

The worst public tragedy I've witnessed was in Boston, when from a distance I saw a brick wall fall on a company of firemen. Some, with a great shout, got away, but even the leap that they made while the rest crumpled is blurred as a memory compared to the images of two old men whom I knew very slightly at the time. Mr. Kate wrote cookbooks in the winter and hired out as a cook on a private yacht during the warm months. His other love, besides cooking, was opera, and he lived in a room shaped like a shoebox that cost him eight dollars a week. He served himself candlelit meals on a folding table and concocted all of his recipes on a hotplate set in the sink. By contrast, Mr. Hurth, although a somewhat less cultivated man, was an alumnus of Brown University and lived in a large ground-floor room in the same house. He had ruined himself in a scandal in St. Louis, where he had been a businessman, but that was all I learned. What he'd done next was to come to Boston and throw himself on the old-fashioned, private or "Christian" charity, as it used to be called, of a roommate from college, though thirty years had passed. He was a pleasant subdued man ordinarily, swinging from sweet to vaguely hangdog, but he was a drinker, and so this benefactor no longer asked him to Newton Centre for Thanksgiving because he was likely to break the furniture. When he did, he'd leave his glasses behind by mistake so that he'd have to go back out again for a whole second festival of apologies. Through charitable intercession, Mr. Hurth was on the payroll of the John Hancock Insurance Company, being listed on the books as a claims investigator, though actually (charity compounding charity) his single duty was to work for the United Fund once a year on a loan basis. The campaign was a brief one, but he was a bitter, floundering functionary, faced with his fate if his drinking should snap off his last sticks of presence and re-spectability.

As I say, next to the memory of two nodding acquaint-ances the death of some distant firemen is small potatoes. I was reminded of that catastrophe the other night for the first time in years while watching a fire on Third Avenue. Here in the bigger city one is witness to such a cataract of appalling happenings that they pass remembering. I saw a man who had just been burned out of his apartment turned away from a hotel in the neighborhood because he had a little blacking on him, although the shock and fear stood in his eyes. "Sure, there was a fire there, all right," the manager told me with a laugh. "I never take them in, those victims. They're dirty and they're scared to death. They're not worth the nuisance."

He was a modern, casual villain, however, impartial, just the kind who is not memorable. I came upon a much less gratuitous drama a few days afterwards. A child of two or three had been stuck inside one of those all-glass phone booths with a spring door which cannot be opened except by a grown person because of where the handle is placed. The world was passing—this was on the open street—but he was feeling his way around the glass in gathering panic, trying to find an escape route, reaching up and reaching down. Every few seconds he let out a thin, fluting scream so pure in pitch that it was hardly human; it was *pre*-human. You could see him thinking, learning, recording discoveries. He reached for the phone, but that was too high up; he thumped each pane of glass, searching for the door, and pounded on the metal frame, and screamed to find whether screaming would work. He was boxed into his terror, and you could see him grow older by leaps and bounds. I'm just this month a new father, so I was as transfixed as if he were my child. His governess or baby-sitter, baby-walker, or whatever she was, a short shadowy woman such as you might see manning a subway change booth, was standing right next to the glass, apparently feasting her eyes. Whether it was supposed to be a "punishment" or merely a pleasure fest, the child was too frightened by now to notice her.

Maybe our cruelty will save us. At least the cruel do pay attention, and the woman would probably have let him out before the crowd got around to hearing him. She had moved to the door, looking down at him intently as he pushed on the glass. I was seething, partly because I found that some of the woman's sexual excitement had communicated itself to me, which was intolerable, and partly because my cowardice in not interfering was equally outrageous. We've all become reluctant to stop and stick our noses in—a man is run over by a Breakstone cream-cheese truck and we pass quickly by. But cowardice was what it was in this particular event, since even under happy circumstances I stutter and it requires an enormous gearing up of nerve for me to step into a public fracas on the street. I strangle; I can't speak at all and must either use my hands on the stranger or gag and quaver, unable to put two words together. The seams of human nature frighten me in this regard, and the whole confrontation ethic of the sixties, much as I have entered into it on occasion, gives me nightmare visions because I have no conventional means of battling. I see myself as unable to protest in words to the person whose behavior has angered me and so using my hands on him; then just as unable to explain myself to the crowd that gathers, but only shuddering and stuttering; and then in court again enforcedly silent, dependent on the empathy or telepathic capacities of the people who are there to convey my side of the controversy.

Weaving like a nauseous moose, I was working my way toward her, when the woman, with a glance at me, pushed the door of the booth open, reached inside, and pulled the boy to her and walked away. In effect, I was let off, because only an exceptional well-doer would have tracked the woman down from that point on and questioned her about her psyche.

However, there are times one isn't let off, when one's very humanity hangs at issue and perhaps my specific problems with my stutter are an epitome of what each of us meets. Once in northern New England when I was snowshoeing, a hunter started shooting at me, really only to scare me, pinging with his .22 in my immediate vicinity. I was on an open hillside which I'd already realized was too slippery to climb, but as long as I kept scrabbling there in silence on the ice, like an animal in trouble, he was going to keep on pinging. Because a stutterer's every impulse is to stutter softly, unobtrusively, it's twice as hard to shout one's way through a stutter as to wedge through in quiet tones; but from the sheer imperatives of survival I shouted, "I CAN SEE YOU!" I shouted it

11

several times again, although I couldn't see him; he was in the woods. I was insisting and reiterating that I was a human being: if I could get that message across to him he would stop shooting at me. It was even worse than my conception of a courtroom trial because this was one of those rare emergencies when we can't trust to all our faculties to operate together for us—the movements of our hands, our youth or age, our manner and expression—some compensating for the inadequacies of the others. I had to go to bat with my speaking abilities and nothing else. So I shouted to him that I could see him, by which I meant I was a man, and he stopped shooting.

More recently, I was on a tiny Danish island off the coast of Sweden, wandering around some seventeenth-century fortifications and the walled town, now a huddled fishing village. I had sat on the sea wall to watch the cloud action but was distracted by the spectacle below me of a boy mistreating a wild duck. Oddly enough, many times an incident where a person, rather than an animal, is being mauled and manhandled is easier to shrug off. The fact that he's a person complicates the case. As an on-looker you can see, for example, that he has gotten himself drunk and let his guard down, lost his dignity, talked out of turn. But the duck, with its wings clipped, presumably, was only trying to run away. The boy would catch it, pummel it and grip it tightly, trundling it about. Finally I got off my bench and went over and told him falteringly to cut that out. Many Danes speak English, but he was twelve or so and he may not have understood me. Like a mirror of myself, he stared at me without trying to say a word. Then he squeezed the duck again hard in both hands. My bugaboo about trying to explain myself to strangers rose in me, along with my indignation. Instead of looking for a local fellow to translate and take over, I lifted the duck from his arms, and with the sense of right and doom that I have dreaded in foreseeing a confrontation on the street, carried it down the stairs of the sea wall and released it on the beach. The boy ran for help; the duck paddled into the waves; I climbed to the promenade and started walking as deliberately as I could toward the small boat which had brought me to the island.

Uncannily soon, before I'd gone a dozen yards, practically the whole male populace was on the scene. "Hey! Turn around!" they yelled. I took another couple of steps away and then did so. They told me very plainly in English that they were going to throw me over the sea wall. They said the duck had been rescued by the boys of the island—their sons—after it had swum through an oil slick and almost drowned. Now, because of what I'd done, it really *was* about to drown, and when it went under, they would toss me over. This was not spoken in joking tones, and I could see the duck getting heavier in the water; its feathers, though as tidy to the eye as a healthy duck's feathers, had no buoyancy. Meanwhile, I'd fallen into something like what a prizefighter would call a clinch by refusing to acknowledge by any sign that I understood what was being said to me. It is a psychological necessity that when you punish somebody he understand the reason why. Even if he doesn't accept the guilty finding, you must explain to him why you are punishing him or you can't do it. So while they could scarcely contain their frustration, my face displayed bewilderment; I kept pretending to grope to understand. I was doing this instinctively, of course, and as their first impetus to violence passed, I found myself acting out with vehemence how I had seen the boy mistreat the duck. The men, who wanted at the least to take a poke at me, watched doubtfully, but there was a Coast Guardsman, an off-islander, who seemed to be arguing in Danish on my behalf. Another man went down to where the duck was swimming and reached out; the duck perceiving itself to be sinking, had moved cautiously closer to shore. And when the duck was saved I was saved; I only had the island's boys waiting for me in the embrasures of the wall.

Yet this quite comic misadventure, when every dread came real—I couldn't say a single word to save my life—was just as numbing as those ninety-five squat jumps at Fort Dix—only later was it terrifying. And in a way it makes up for the memories I have as a teenager of watching flocks of bats murdered with brooms and frogs tormented—moments when I didn't interfere, but giggled ruefully to keep my popularity and stifle my outcries.

Sociology progresses; the infant mortality rate among Negroes goes down. Nevertheless we know that if the announcement were made that there was going to be a public hanging in Central Park, Sheep Meadow would be crowded with spectators, like Tyburn mall. Sometimes at night my standing lamp shapes itself into an observant

14

phantom figure which takes a position next to my bed. It doesn't threaten me directly, and I stretch out to clutch its throat with careful anger. My final grab bumps the lamp over. This electric phantom is a holdover from my vivid night demons when I was eight or ten. I never saw them outright, thank the Lord, but for years I fell asleep facing the wall to avoid beholding my destruction. I'd "whisper," as I called it, when I went to bed, telling myself an installment of a round-robin story, and when the installment was over I'd wait for the demons, until I fell asleep. Later, just as invariably, I faced the outer room so I could see them come and have warning to fight. Such archaisms in our minds are not an unmixed evil, however, because they link us to humanity and to our history as human beings. My wife says every man she's been familiar with would smell his socks at night before he went to bed: just a whiff—each sock, not only one. I do this too, although the smell has been of no intrinsic interest to me for twenty years. The smell of each sock checks precisely with the other one and smells as vital as pigs do. Maybe it reassures us that we're among the living still. We need to know. In the fifties I also liked the smell of air pollution. I didn't think of it as air pollution then—nobody did—but as the smell of industry and the highways I hitchhiked on, the big-shouldered America I loved.

In 1943 George Orwell said the problem of the times was the decay in the belief in personal immortality. Several French novelists had turned existentialist and several English novelists Catholic (possibly the same reaction), while he himself, like many of the more likable writers, had adopted a hardy humanist's masculine skepticism. Twenty-odd years later, the problem appears only to have grown more piercing, though it is not put into the same terms. You can't have as many people walking around as there are now and still simply see them as chips off the divine lodestone. Nor is the future *1984*: that's too succinct. At first the new nuclear bullying, the new technocracy, made mere survival more the point, because we wanted to be sure of surviving here on earth before we worried about heaven. Lately, instead the talk has been about overpopulation, and city people have started venturing to the outback, buying acreage with all the premonitory fervor of Noah sawing logs. Everyone wants space to breathe; the character of city life has drastically deteriorated, and there's no questioning the statistics, just as there used to be no questioning the odds that eventually a nuclear war was going to penetrate our precautions through that old fontanel of existence: human mix-up.

When we say that enough is enough, that we have enough people on hand now for any good purpose, we mean that the divine spark has become something of a conflagration, besides an embarrassment of riches. We're trying to make a start at sorting the riches, buying Edwardian clothes but also Volkswagens, and settling down to the process of zoning the little land there is. As we also begin to cogitate on how the quality of life can be improved, we may be in for a religious revival, too. It's a natural beginning, and faddism will probably swing that way, and after all, we *are* extraordinary—we're so extraordinary we're everywhere. Next to the new mysticisms, old-fashioned, run-of-the-mill religion is not so hard to swallow. The difficulty will be how we regard individual people, a question which involves not only whether we think we're immortal but whether we think they are. The crowded impatience of suburb-city living doesn't often evoke intimations of other people's immortality, and neither do the hodge-podge leveling procedures of a modern democracy. So much of the vigor of the Victorian church, for instance, grew out of the contrast between its members and the raw, destitute brown masses who covered the rest of the globe. Among an elite, self-congratulatory minority even the greatest of attributes—immortality—seemed plausible.

But maybe I'm being overly sour. We have wiped tigers off the earth and yet our children hear as much about the symbolism of tigers as children did in the old days. And next to the subway station I use there is a newsdealer who was blinded in Orwell's war, the Spanish War, in the mountains behind Motril. He wears the aura of a revolutionary volunteer. He dresses bulkily, as if for weather at the front, and rigs canvas around his hut as neatly as a soldier's tent. Not one of your meek blind men, he's on his feet most of the day, especially in tough weather, pacing, marching, standing tall. He's gray and grim, hard and spare, and doubtless lives surrounded by the companions that he had in the Sierra Nevada. But he's too bluff and energetic to be a museum piece. If you help him cross the street you get the rough edge of his tongue. He searches for the lamppost with his cane like a tennis player swinging backhand, and if he loses his bearings and bumps against something, he jerks abruptly back like a cavalier insulted, looking gaunt and fierce. I pity him, but I take note of him; he counts himself among the living. I buy a paper and go home to my newborn baby, who is as intense and focused (to my eye) as a flight of angels dancing on a pinhead.

I don't believe in a god you can pray to, but I do find I believe in God—I do more than I don't. I believe in glee and in the exuberance I feel with friends and animals and in the fields, and in other emotions besides that. Anyway, as we know, it really isn't necessary to see sparks of a grand divinity in someone else to feel with the old immediacy that he is kin; we can evolve a more sophisticated Golden Rule than that. We will be trying to refine and revivify the qualities of life, and the chief stumbling block is that we must somehow reduce the density of people in our own comings and goings without doing it as we do now, which is by simply not seeing them, by registering them as shadows to dodge by on the street. Without degenerating into callousness, we must develop our ability to switch on and off—something analogous to what we do already with body temperature in a harsh world. Generally we'd button up if we were out walking, but when the Breakstone cream-cheese truck ran over an old man, this would be a time when our ancient instinct for cherishing a stranger would spring to being.

I live in a high-rise apartment and keep a pair of field glasses next to the window to use whenever somebody emerges on one of the rooftops nearby. There are ten or fifteen regulars—old people hanging wash, high school kids who have come up into the open to talk where they can be alone. All of them are neighbors to me now, though on the street I probably would turn away from them— even the bathing beauties would not be beauties there. Admittedly I am a bit of a voyeur, as who isn't, but the population density on the rooftops seems about right. In fact, I roused myself not long ago to drive some robbers off a roof across the street by gesticulating sternly. They waved back as they went down the stairs like people who've escaped a fall.

THE
COURAGE OF
TURTLES

Turtles are a kind of bird with the governor turned low. With the same attitude of removal, they cock a glance at what is going on, as if they need only to fly away. Until recently they were also a case of virtue rewarded, at least in the town where I grew up, because, being humble creatures, there were plenty of them. Even when we still had a few bobcats in the woods the local snapping turtles, growing up to forty pounds, were the largest carnivores. You would see them through the amber water, as big as greeny wash basins at the bottom of the pond, until they faded into the inscrutable mud as if they hadn't existed at all.

When I was ten I went to Dr. Green's Pond, a two-acre pond across the road. When I was twelve I walked a mile or so to Taggart's Pond, which was lusher, had big water snakes and a waterfall; and shortly after that I was bicycling way up to the adventuresome vastness of Mud Pond, a lake-sized body of water in the reservoir system

of a Connecticut city, possessed of cat-backed little is-
lands and empty shacks and a forest of pines and hard-
woods along the shore. Otters, foxes and mink left their
prints on the bank; there were pike and perch. As I got
older, the estates and forgotten back lots in town were
parceled out and sold for nice prices, yet, though the
woods had shrunk, it seemed that fewer people walked
in the woods. The new residents didn't know how to find
them. Eventually, exploring, they did find them, and it
required some ingenuity and doubling around on my part
to go for eight miles without meeting someone. I was
grown by now, I lived in New York, and that's what I
wanted on the occasional weekends when I came out.

Since Mud Pond contained drinking water I had felt
confident nothing untoward would happen there. For a
long while the developers stayed away, until the drought
of the mid-1960s. This event, squeezing the edges in,
convinced the local water company that the pond really
wasn't a necessity as a catch basin, however; so they
bulldozed a hole in the earthen dam, bulldozed the banks
to fill in the bottom, and landscaped the flow of water
that remained to wind like an English brook and provide
a domestic view for the houses which were planned. Most
of the painted turtles of Mud Pond, who had been inaccessible as they sunned on their rocks, wound up in boxes
in boys' closets within a matter of days. Their footsteps
in the dry leaves gave them away as they wandered
forlornly. The snappers and the little musk turtles, neither
of whom leave the water except once a year to lay their
eggs, dug into the drying mud for another siege of hot

21

weather, which they were accustomed to doing whenever the pond got low. But this time it was low for good; the mud baked over them and slowly entombed them. As for the ducks, I couldn't stroll in the woods and not feel guilty, because they were crouched beside every stagnant pothole, or were slinking between the bushes with their heads tucked into their shoulders so that I wouldn't see them. If they decided I had, they beat their way up through the screen of trees, striking their wings dangerously, and wheeled about with that headlong, magnificent velocity to locate another poor puddle.

I used to catch possums and black snakes as well as turtles, and I kept dogs and goats. Some summers I worked in a menagerie with the big personalities of the animal kingdom, like elephants and rhinoceroses. I was twenty before these enthusiasms began to wane, and it was then that I picked turtles as the particular animal I wanted to keep in touch with. I was allergic to fur, for one thing, and turtles need minimal care and not much in the way of quarters. They're personable beasts. They see the same colors we do and they seem to see just as well, as one discovers in trying to sneak up on them. In the laboratory they unravel the twists of a maze with the hot-blooded rapidity of a mammal. Though they can't run as fast as a rat, they improve on their errors just as quickly, pausing at each crossroads to look left and right. And they rock rhythmically in place, as we often do, although they are hatched from eggs, not the womb. (A common explanation psychologists give for our pleasure in rocking quietly is that it recapitulates our mother's heartbeat *in utero.*)

Snakes, by contrast, are dryly silent and priapic. They are smooth movers, legalistic, unblinking, and they afford the humor which the humorless do. But they make challenging captives; sometimes they don't eat for months on a point of order—if the light isn't right, for instance. Alligators are sticklers too. They're like war-horses, or German shepherds, and with their bar-shaped, vertical pupils adding emphasis, they have the *idée fixe* of eating, eating, even when they choose to refuse all food and stubbornly die. They delight in tossing a salamander up towards the sky and grabbing him in their long mouths as he comes down. They're so eager that they get the jitters, and they're too much of a proposition for a casual aquarium like mine. Frogs are depressingly defenseless: that moist, extensive back, with the bones almost sticking through. Hold a frog and you're holding its skeleton. Frogs' tasty legs are the staff of life to many animals— herons, raccoons, ribbon snakes—though they themselves are hard to feed. It's not an enviable role to be the staff of life, and after frogs you descend down the evolutionary ladder a big step to fish.

Turtles cough, burp, whistle, grunt and hiss, and produce social judgments. They put their heads together amicably enough, but then one drives the other back with the suddenness of two dogs who have been conversing in tones too low for an onlooker to hear. They pee in fear when they're first caught, but exercise both pluck and optimism in trying to escape, walking for hundreds of yards within the confines of their pen, carrying the weight of that cumbersome box on legs which are cruelly positioned for walking. They don't feel that the contest is unfair; they keep plugging, rolling like sailorly souls —a bobbing, infirm gait, a brave, sea-legged momentum —stopping occasionally to study the lay of the land. For me, anyway, they manage to contain the rest of the animal world. They can stretch out their necks like a giraffe, or loom underwater like an apocryphal hippo. They browse on lettuce thrown on the water like a cow moose which is partly submerged. They have a penguin's alertness, combined with a build like a Brontosaurus when they rise up on tiptoe. Then they hunch and ponderously lunge like a grizzly going forward.

Baby turtles in a turtle bowl are a puzzle in geometrics. They're as decorative as pansy petals, but they are also self-directed building blocks, propping themselves on one another in different arrangements, before upending the tower. The timid individuals turn fearless, or vice versa. If one gets a bit arrogant he will push the others off the rock and afterwards climb down into the water and cling to the back of one of those he has bullied, tickling him with his hind feet until he bucks like a bronco. On the other hand, when this same milder-mannered fellow isn't exerting himself, he will stare right into the face of the sun for hours. What could be more lionlike? And he's at home in or out of the water and does lots of metaphysical tilting. He sinks and rises, with an infinity of levels to choose from; or, elongating himself, he climbs out on the land again to perambulate, sits boxed in his box, and finally slides back in the water, submerging into dreams.

I have five of these babies in a kidney-shaped bowl. The hatchling, who is a painted turtle, is not as large as the top joint of my thumb. He eats chicken gladly. Other foods he will attempt to eat but not with sufficient perseverance to succeed because he's so little. The yellow-bellied terrapin is probably a yearling, and he eats salad voraciously, but no meat, fish or fowl. The Cumberland terrapin won't touch salad or chicken but eats fish and all of the meats except for bacon. The little snapper, with a black crenelated shell, feasts on any kind of meat, but rejects greens and fish. The fifth of the turtles is African. I acquired him only recently and don't know him well. A mottled brown, he unnerves the green turtles, dragging their food off to his lairs. He doesn't seem to want to be green—he bites the algae off his shell, hanging meanwhile at daring, steep, head-first angles.

The snapper was a Ferdinand until I provided him with deeper water. Now he snaps at my pencil with his downturned and fearsome mouth, his swollen face like a napalm victim's. The Cumberland has an elliptical red mark on the side of his green-and-yellow head. He is benign by nature and ought to be as elegant as his scientific name (*Pseudemys scripta elegans*), except he has contracted a disease of the air bladder which has permanently inflated it; he floats high in the water at an undignified slant and can't go under. There may have been internal bleeding, too, because his carapace is stained along its ridge. Unfortunately, like flowers, baby turtles often die. Their mouths fill up with a white fungus and their lungs with pneumonia. Their organs clog up from the rust in the water, or diet troubles, and, like a dying man's, their eyes and heads become too prominent. Toward the end, the edge of the shell becomes flabby as felt and folds around them like a shroud.

While they live they're like puppies. Although they're vivacious, they would be a bore to be with all the time, so I also have an adult wood turtle about six inches long. Her shell is the equal of any seashell for sculpturing, even a Cellini shell; it's like an old, dusty, richly engraved medallion dug out of a hillside. Her legs are salmon-orange bordered with black and protected by canted, heroic scales. Her plastron—the bottom shell—is splotched like a margay cat's coat, with black ocelli on a yellow background. It is convex to make room for the female organs inside, whereas a male's would be concave to help him fit tightly on top of her. Altogether, she exhibits every camouflage color on her limbs and shells. She has a turtleneck neck, a tail like an elephant's, wise old pachydermous hind legs and the face of a turkey—except that when I carry her she gazes at the passing ground with a hawk's eyes and mouth. Her feet fit to the fingers of my hand, one to each one, and she rides looking down. She can walk on the floor in perfect silence, but usually she lets her shell knock portentously, like a footstep, so that she resembles some grand, concise, slow-moving id. But if an earthworm is presented, she jerks swiftly ahead, poises above it and strikes like a mongoose, consuming it with wild vigor. Yet she will climb on my lap to eat bread or boiled eggs.

If put into a creek, she swims like a cutter, nosing forward to intercept a strange turtle and smell him. She drifts with the current to go downstream, maneuvering behind a rock when she wants to take stock, or sinking to the nether levels, while bubbles float up. Getting out, choosing her path, she will proceed a distance and dig into a pile of humus, thrusting herself to the coolest layer at the bottom. The hole closes over her until it's as small as a mouse's hole. She's not as aquatic as a musk turtle, not quite as terrestrial as the box turtles in the same woods, but because of her versatility she's marvelous, she's everywhere. And though she breathes the way we breathe, with scarcely perceptible movements of her chest, sometimes instead she pumps her throat ruminatively, like a pipe smoker sucking and puffing. She waits and blinks, pumping her throat, turning her head, then sets off like a loping tiger in slow motion, hurdling the jungly lumber, the pea vine and twigs. She estimates angles so well that when she rides over the rocks, sliding down a drop-off with her rugged front legs extended, she has the grace of a rodeo mare.

But she's well off to be with me rather than at Mud Pond. The other turtles have fled—those that aren't baked into the bottom. Creeping up the brooks to sad, constricted marshes, burdened as they are with that box on their backs, they're walking into a setup where all their enemies move thirty times faster than they. It's like the nightmare most of us have whimpered through, where we are weighted down disastrously while trying to flee; fleeing our home ground, we try to run.

I've seen turtles in still worse straits. On Broadway, in New York, there is a penny arcade which used to sell baby terrapins that were scrawled with bon mots in enamel paint, such as KISS ME BABY. The manager turned out to be a wholesaler as well, and once I asked him whether he had any larger turtles to sell. He took me upstairs to a loft room devoted to the turtle business. There were desks for the paper work and a series of racks that held shallow tin bins atop one another, each with several hundred babies crawling around in it. He was a smudgy-complexioned, serious fellow and he did have a few adult terrapins, but I was going to school and wasn't actually planning to buy; I'd only wanted to see them. They were aquatic turtles, but here they went without water, presumably for weeks, lurching about in those dry bins like handicapped citizens, living on gumption. An easel where the artist worked stood in the middle of the floor. She had a palette and a clip attachment for fastening the babies in place. She wore a smock and a beret, and was homely, short and eccentric-looking, with funny black hair, like some of the ladies who show their paintings in Washington Square in May. She had a cold, she was smoking, and her hand wasn't very steady, although she worked quickly enough. The smile that she produced for me would have looked giddy if she had been happier, or drunk. Of course the turtles' doom was sealed when she painted them, because their bodies inside would continue to grow but their shells would not. Gradually, invisibly, they would be crushed. Around us their bellies—two thousand belly shells—rubbed on the bins with a mournful, momentous hiss.

Somehow there were so many of them I didn't rescue one. Years later, however, I was walking on First Avenue when I noticed a basket of living turtles in front of a fish store. They were as dry as a heap of old bones in the sun; nevertheless, they were creeping over one another gimpily, doing their best to escape. I looked and was touched to discover that they appeared to be wood turtles, my favorites, so I bought one. In my apartment I looked closer and realized that in fact this was a diamond-back terrapin, which was bad news. Diamondbacks are tidewater turtles from brackish estuaries, and I had no sea water to keep him in. He spent his days thumping interminably against the baseboards, pushing for an opening through the wall. He drank thirstily but would not eat and had none of the hearty, accepting qualities of wood turtles. He was morose, paler in color, sleeker and more Oriental in the carved ridges and rings that formed his shell. Though I felt sorry for him, finally I found his unrelenting presence exasperating. I carried him, strugglinging in a paper bag, across town to the Morton Street Pier on the Hudson. It was August but gray and windy. He was very surprised when I tossed him in; for the first time in our association, I think, he was afraid. He looked afraid as he bobbed about on top of the water, looking up at me from ten feet below. Though we were both accustomed to his resistance and rigidity, seeing him still

29

pitiful, I recognized that I must have done the wrong thing. At least the river was salty, but it was also bottomless; the waves were too rough for him, and the tide was coming in, bumping him against the pilings underneath the pier. Too late, I realized that he wouldn't be able to swim to a peaceful inlet in New Jersey, even if he could figure out which way to swim. But since, short of diving in after him, there was nothing I could do, I walked away.

THE
WAR IN THE
WOODS

Even in the present day there are a few individuals scattered about the world who have a power of communicating with animals that corresponds, perhaps, to ESP. It is more easily believable, however, since we can see that animals themselves, both wild and domestic, communicate with each other across the barriers of species and of habitat. Bits of filler about these people appear occasionally in the understrata of the news: some herdsman or charcoal burner in a corner of Afghanistan, a leopard hunter, an elephant driver, a race-track groom. The best animal trainers undoubtedly have had this special capacity along with their daring and verve, but more often it seems to be a man who does not put the gift to any especially profitable use, who lives humbly, as snake charmers and village madmen do, and whose insights bring him as much sadness as gaiety—whose allegiances are torn. I've known trainers who at least were acquainted with the Berlitz equivalent of animal talk, the phrase-book forms—how to arrest the attention of a wildebeest or comfort a whistling swan—and once I heard a firsthand description of the real article, a wandering fellow who appeared, Pied Piper-fashion, at a zoo-animal dealer's and asked for a job as a cage hand. He went into all the cages and soothed the pandas who were just off the boat, encouraged the toucans, and babbled softly to the llamas, gesturing, mumbling, making small sounds. He lived in the sheds with the animals for as long as he stayed, and was a queer, inoffensive, skinny person of no recognizable age, with a timid, energetic stoop like Danny Kaye's. Animals of every type hurried sociably to meet him at the bars when he drew near, following him as far as their cages allowed: an immediate reaction from the first day. He was invaluable as an employee. The creatures who were on hunger strikes took food, and none of them injured themselves in struggling to escape while they were being crated. And yet the prison-like routine saddened him—being warden, and then shipping them off when telegrams from around the country arrived. Soon he was on the road again, with his suitcase.

This was thirty or forty years ago. The chance for such a singular changeling to spring out of the throng has lessened as the rest of us see fewer animals, have less to do with animals—even a farm boy is becoming quite a rarity. The animals we do know something about are manufactured as commodities: our million steers like cardboard cutouts and our frenetic, force-fed hens. Most of the dogs in the pet shops come out of virtual factories now, and dogs are notable because they go three-fourths of the way in preserving a semblance of an interchange between animal and man. They go so far as to learn English, they cringe on cue and look laudatory. For reasons that are as intense as they are inexplicable, dogs really want to reach us, and when they do, our kindness or our wizardry, our amazing *imaginations,* bring them joy.

Interestingly, though, some of the wild animals make advances to us too—like porpoises and the primates and certain birds. Campers often have a camp weasel or mouse hanging about, and mountain lions on many occasions have poked their heads into a tent and sniffed the sleeper in his sleeping bag, peaceably and curious— the big tracks came and went—or bounded invitingly around while he pulled the eiderdown over his head. Both the Indian tribes and early settlers developed legends of the friendliness of mountain lions to travelers and children which, if exaggerated, must still have contained a core of truth. In the southwestern U.S., Indians even revered them—it was believed that their urine, in drying, hardened into a precious stone—and in Argentina they were known as "the Christian's friend." Wolves did not establish such a reputation for curiosity about human beings, but wolves are related to dogs, and the ferocious Russian wolf is outvoted in folklore by numerous Mowgli-prototype stories of wolves on the Indian subcontinent, in Rome and Italy, and even in Vermont. (In 1780, Ethan Allen, leading a search party, found two lost little girls, aged five and seven, who after forty-eight hours were in the company of a timber wolf.) Of course, among the duchies of the animal kingdom there are plenty of creatures who feel no affinity for men at all, or for kinkajous either. Still, if they have backbones, they do perhaps feel an affiliation with the pulse of life itself. Reptiles eat with great relish, preferring twisting, living prey, the livelier the better; and recently a small boy, washed overboard in the Atlantic, was rescued hours later clinging to a large sea turtle which was swimming on the surface at a stately, level pace. Presumably this act of keeping him afloat was not an act of mercy on the turtle's part (though some turtles do know about "drowning"—they drown ducks, catching them from below by the feet and pulling them underwater). The turtle probably just felt comfortable in company with the boy, animal-to-animal, felt a sort of rudimentary comradeship, so that it made no objection to being utilized as a life ring.

Bears are not as chummy, however; hence our word "bearish." They are exorbitant eaters. They must sleep for six months at a stretch and they must eat enormously in order to be able to sleep, so their main connection with people is that they like most of the foods that people do. The strangely delicate or lonely accord a puma gives evidence of feeling as it touches its nose to a man's nose as he lies sleeping, having circled a deserted lake to reach his camp, or when it follows him for half a dozen miles, placing each foot exactly in his footprints and playing hopscotch-like games—this is not the style of a bluff bruiser like a bear. Bears are lugs, and they have dim eyesight but superb ears and a superlative nose, maybe the best on earth. They're brainy too, and they've distinguished between their front and hind limbs so long and diligently that the paws have acquired different shapes. They really do love food, eating ingeniously, omnivorously, such items as horse plums, wild apples, parsnips, shadberries, lupine, Solomon's seal, Epilobiums, chipmunks, beetles, rhubarb, and watercress and spawning fish and carrion meat. Zoos feed them loaves of whole-grained bread baked with molasses and supplements. Naturally they're broader-beamed in the rear than in the front, though since they don't often kill game (polar bears are an exception), their mouths are modest in dimension. They have a good set of teeth tucked inside but the mouth isn't sharklike, isn't proportioned like cleavers and axes, and they don't eat desperately, the way shrews do; their timetable is leisurely; they fatten like a woodchuck, moving from feast to feast as between cheerful surprises, scooping fruit, pruning the branches with their paws. They like our leavings too, if they can find a dump, and people who eat bears report that their meat tastes much the same as our meat used to taste to cannibals, or like the other famous omnivore, the pig. Bears may be tall and rangily built or stocky, squat, and with a pot, the short bear perhaps heavier than the large-looking fellow, just like the many varieties of man; and with their overall man shape and size, their spirited minds, their manlike wails and grunts, they have intrigued people for centuries. In societies where they didn't serve as a manhood test, they were captured alive and employed as crude gladiators in underground arenas, fighting dogs and bulls. The gypsies made them dance for coins, training them by torturing their feet with heated irons. Grizzly Adams, the mountainman, slept with his bears on cold nights (as some gypsies must have), and bear rugs were standard bedding throughout the northern hemisphere at times—they're still *de rigueur* for "dens."

Bears are fairly casual about how they pass the winter. Protected from the snow by their warm coats, they just roll in under a fallen spruce when food gets short, pulling a few boughs over themselves, as often as they take the trouble to search out a cave. They choose the north side of a mountain so that the sun won't melt them out, but don't necessarily trek back to the same area year after year. They hibernate singly; cubs are born to a mother every other winter while she lies in a doze, waking only to bite the umbilical cords. Sometimes a woodsman on snowshoes will notice a rhythmic succession of puffs of steam rising from a tiny hole in the cover of snow and know that he's passing a sleeping bear. It's as personal as an experience I once had, of finding a grizzly's tracks in mud alongside the Bowron River so fresh the water was still trickling into them.

Bears are a kind of shadow of man, a tracery or etching of him—as mutes and schizophrenics and idiots sometimes are—a view of him if he'd stayed in the woods, among the rocks, instead of becoming community-minded. The "wild-man-of-the-woods" whom northwestern Indians fear wears a bear's shape, though he is humanoid in his sexual proclivities—he catches Indian girls; his face and his coat are a mask. Even a real bear's

36

face is quite a mask, from the standpoint of an animal trainer. The stolid, terse muzzle, the small, practically hidden eyes, the thick, short fur overgrowing the features, give the trainer no window to the bear's emotions such as he has in a lion's great eyes. A tiger's white *whiskers*, as flexile as they are, are worth a good deal toward saving the trainer from harm, and the expressive lip, the subtle, definitive index of roars are worth much more— not to mention the tail and the curl of the toes. By comparison, a bear's lips hardly move, he has no whiskers to mention, no particular tail, and blocks for toes, and though he may occasionally chop his jaws before attacking, emitting a low breathy growl, often he won't. His hasty antics when he meets you on the road and prepares to make good his escape cause you to wonder which way he actually intends to go; and a trained bear, losing the restraining element of fear, becomes even more bouncy, cryptic and clownish.

Grizzlies do roar and *waw* and make all the faces of Baal, but grizzlies have not been trained in recent times and they can pretty well be written off, relegated to the paleontologist. In a few spots they are managing to make a stand, feeding on the moose that hunters wound—inland grizzlies with bush to roam. The polar bears—"sea bears"—are in a worse predicament, being hunted with airplanes. Part of the bears' plight may be our own, although they need so much more space that they are being squeezed off the earth sooner than we. The black bears are more apropos, being gerrymandering scroungers who manage to fit into any dab of forest that presents itself; in any few square miles of tangled growth they can set up house, eating beechnuts and leopard frogs, and render themselves almost indiscernible. But in those woods, that concealed bear is like the mercury in a thermometer or the bean in a jumping bean. He moves so fast (when once he moves) when you come upon him that you know he's the forest's reason for being, or the nearest thing to a reason for being that you will ever see.

I talked to a man who had lain helplessly under a grizzly. He was living in Manson Creek, a settlement of twenty citizens in north-central British Columbia where the mail was delivered every second week. He was a clear-faced, well-built, balding man in his late thirties, and a disaffected philosopher, a man who had read mightily on his own but had no one to talk to, who had left Indiana University, estranged from his wife. He read half the night by the light of a Coleman lamp and wrote during the day, hoping to finish a book; but he liked the rough life, skiing out to look at wolf kills, and though he worried about his marriage, so far as I could tell he was holding up under the pressures of isolation, except that he needed to air his thoughts.

The encounter occurred when he was driving along a dirt road that wound for a couple of hundred miles to a mining camp. He'd stopped his car and climbed down a bank, aiming for a promontory where he hoped to see into a valley. Instead he blundered into a bowl-like depression a dozen yards wide in which a grizzly, waxing fat with the hunting season, was feeding on a moose carcass. The moose had gone there to die and the grizzly's quick nose had found it. The brush was wet, the wind blew loudly in the fellow's face, so that the bear may not have scented him, or may have scented him and waited. At nearly the same instant they saw each other, close up—the bear's head lifting, bloody and aswarm with flies. This shocking sight, really before he could take it in, was followed by the impact of the bear bashing him over. Flung as if hit by a bus, he was not immediately reactive, yet the bear seemed loath to bite him. It lurched and bunched its neck, he said, and swatted at him, raging. Lying on his back, he drew up his feet as a buffer. It was so big he saw it as a shape then, without color, but in the same factual detail as if he were a third party observing. And though its charge had knocked him sprawling, a sort of disgust or revulsion, apparently, a wish not to contact him with its mouth, kept it from grappling him more closely. Reaching around his legs, it raked and gashed him, roaring with fury but reluctant to use its mouth.

He said he'd had no nightmares to confuse his memory of the accident (he thought of it as that); nor did he expect any. And he was not a sentimental man who would falsely anthropomorphize the bear's behavior; he was living in the bush to write a philosophical study and take a breather, not in order to feed the finches. The bear started leaving, but bumped against the moose, lunged over it, then paused, unable to pull itself away, as if the outrage of being interrupted when eating was too obnoxious for it to just be able to back away from him and leave. It seemed "torn," he said—wanting to rush for cover and yet standing in the middle of their little amphitheater, boiling with insult.

When a grizzly mauls a man the real destruction it does is with its mouth: in bedside interviews, people who have been bitten have described the cumulatively catastrophic damage inflicted on them by a series of chomps. Even so, in most cases the man survives; the bear bites near his neck but doesn't quite get there, and runs off, leaving him mauled but alive. This bear, likewise, torn between its obvious abhorrence of approaching my informant and the urge to wreak havoc on him, hesitated, bawling and swaying, chopping its jaws. Finally it attacked again, lacerating his sides, pummeling his arms when they were interposed, reaching around his boots as he lay balled up on his back and kicked and, deaf to himself, probably shrieked. Outweighing him by several hundred pounds, it growled like a bass banshee, but it was so absolutely aghast at their proximity—holding its face away as if at the stench of him—that its blows were just tentative. Afterwards the doctor found dozens of scratches on him but not many substantial hurts. One claw had cut through his wallet and through the money in the wallet. And for my friend, as well, once the first terrible glimpse and charge were over, the really ghastly horror of the experience was the matter of scent. He could avoid watching the bear but he couldn't escape its smell. And, as soberly, methodically, as he was speaking to me, he couldn't describe it either, except as odious suffocation—violent, vile aversion. It was not like pyorrhea, nor like a garbage pit; it was everything fetid and scarifying and strangling rolled into one disgusting cloud which was more frightening than all the injuries and pain. Hunters call the smell cabbagy and go wild with excitement when they catch a whiff, but he was lying right underneath the mouth, which was its source.

If bears usually go to such considerable lengths to avoid our company, why do we search out theirs? It seems to be in order to count coup. Even at the taxidermist's, where the bears arrive daily in trucks, you notice that the youngster who is in charge of rugged work, like sawing off their heads, does it with a Homeric zest. "You see how we treat you?" he tells them, rolling their corpses and slapping the contorted mouths. A hunter after grizzly must spend a thousand dollars or more in transportation costs simply to get to grizzly country, and in New England bear hunters are usually bear hunters by chance, the bears are so wary and shy. Only about three per cent of those killed in Vermont, for instance, have been inveigled to their deaths with bait. Ten per cent have been tracked down with hounds, and the rest fall prize to hunters who "stand and stalk," in the official Fish and Wildlife phrase, which means that they're out in the woods carrying a gun, maybe after deer, when they happen to pitch upon a bear.

I've gone on several hound hunts, as well as stand-and-stalk hunts and ambushes. But hound hunts are the realistic ones; also, the hounds, being agents, interest me. Grizzlies have seldom been hunted with hounds (though some of the Indians did, adding themselves to the pack to give it extra authority), and even in running down black bears, which are neither so dangerous nor the size of a King Kong, the first problem is finding dogs gritty enough to hold the bear—make him come to bay. The smell is strong, goodness knows, and the bear, though big and vital and thick-skinned, cannot run faster than a dog, especially in the fall, when he is necessarily fattening himself (very old bears die during hibernation because they weren't able to fatten up enough). Therefore if a bear is lurking around, no worthy hunting dog will have much difficulty scenting him or catching up; the feat is to conquer him and send him scrambling up a tree. When they contact the bear, most dogs stop dead a moment, then promptly swing around and dash for home. Some sportsmen call a bear hunt successful if they can only catch their hounds by the end of the day. On Monday mornings, the local radio stations broadcast appeals for "a Walker hound lost on the Long Trail under Hazen's Notch."

Besides the Walker breed, others that can be worked on bear are Blueticks, Black-and-tans, Redbones and Plotts; and Airedale blood is sometimes bred into a pack for extra grit. Basically, there are two jobs—the strike dog's and the hold dog's. Working alone, the strike dog finds a cold trail and works at it till he approaches the bear and makes him feel uneasy enough to get up out of his noon bed. He needs to have an excellent nose and an instructive voice which carries well, and to be a dog of self-sufficient sense but not too fast, since the rest of the pack is not released until he is full-out on a fresh track. The hold dogs, fast as fickle lightning in a scrimmage, specialists at "pulling fur," are the fighters who will risk their skin. The bear may run for twenty miles altogether, fighting wherever he can set his back against a ledge or a big tree and only running on again when the hunters draw near. States like New York and Pennsylvania have outlawed trailing bears with hounds because they think the animals may have a hard enough time as it is; and the contest does include a quite peculiar proxy element. Besides the metaphorically turncoat nature of the dog's role—who leads his master to any creature, to a woodcock or a slew of truffles—there is a mameluke-style madness too. The dog is kept chained the whole year to focus all his personality on his brief spurts of work, then let loose for a few weekends in the fall to run and run, trying to crowd in a lifetime's excitement before he's chained up for another year. Dogs are very much like other animals (watch a mother training her pups), except for the one central dislocation that they are no longer able to collect their food. Even hunting dogs, when lost and starving in the woods, can't, and so with this linchpin removed, they're like a Chinese girl hobbling on bound feet for her husband's accommodation, or like the birds which feudal young ladies kept, which didn't require caging because the front of their bill was broken off—they couldn't pick up their own food from the ground and only ate from their possessor's hand.

A bear's about the biggest game. Foxes are for horsemen in open country, and coon hunting is not much of a sport; it just boils down to watching the dogs do a job. The raccoon doesn't run very far before climbing a tree once he is chased in earnest; the dogs only have to un- ravel the evidence of where he is. Bobcats are a better quarry because the chase is more complex. The cat has a poor nose but compensates for the handicap with his eyes and ears, and will slip through the boondocks for many miles, using marsh ice and deadfalls to confuse the scent—the females are said to be harder to tree, as if they valued their lives more hotly. Bears, being so large, so manlike anatomically and yet lusciously furred, wily and yet raunchy, "understandable" but possessing a beast's stamina, are way ahead of the other North American game animals as prospective adversaries. They can kill dogs—they're brutes—but since their pleasures, their sense of play and diet, their cast of instincts, their strategy or reasoning, are within a realm which we can reach by an effort of empathy, we can pretend that we're Jack- and-the-Beanstalk and they're a personal sort of Goliath, which is both fun and very bolstering.

The Vermont season extends three months, starting September 1. During September a bear's coat is so flimsily rooted and thin that you can see right through it, so a scrupulous hunter doesn't shoot the bears he runs across but restricts himself to training and conditioning his dogs for the grueling, more businesslike pursuits of Octo- ber, when the woods still belong to him. In November the deer hunters are everywhere and any hound is shot on sight. This bloodless September stuff suits me fine, however. My companion is Paul Doyle, a gentlemanly, diffidently chatty insurance man in the town of Orleans, Vt., whose engrossing hobby is chasing bears. As a hunter he is compelling and leaderly, and young men gather about him; he's in his forties and has a family of four daughters but no sons. He's a good-humored, resourceful talker, making it all as individualized as he can. He talks about the game as though they were a bunch of comic understudies for mankind, a shrewd and shadowy tribe whose delight is playing jokes and tricks: if the bugger outsmarts him and the dogs, that day he gets away. He's dry, doubting, but rather fond when mentioning the residents of the many farms we pass as we roar around by truck on the dirt roads towards various hunting grounds. He receives frequent calls from people who think that a coon is threatening their chickens or their corn, or who claim they've seen a bobcat's track. The tracks are often illusory and the wind may have blown down the corn, but it gives him a chance to chat a while and maybe write some insurance. For eighteen years he himself farmed, and he grew up on one. Besides, he enjoys people and is a man whose hunting is primarily combative, the dogs being deputies and proxies. He's not the type of hunter who prefers the company of animals and who would just as soon sneak across somebody's woodlot on the way to a kill as first go to the house and get acquainted with the owner.

Here are three hunts. Doyle, I and his three dogs, which are a Plott-and-Bluetick cross, rode in an International Scout, a jeeplike truck, and Bob Cody and Eric Gilfallen, sidekicks of his, rode in their own vehicles behind, each with a pair of dogs. Eric, who brought along his little son, is a trainee for IBM, a sloping-nosed, blue-eyed fellow just growing out of being callow, a modernized young man whom I tended to like better each time we met. Bob Cody, a bus driver in Burlington, puts up a tent on Doyle's lawn on weekends for the sake of these hunts. He's a kidder, a staunch-looking, husky person who tilts and fusses with his square-billed cap like a coach giving signals.

On the first hunt, we went to the Duck Pond Road in the township of Glover. It's a defunct jigsaw road, scarcely navigable, that twists past abandoned farmsteads and log houses for a dozen miles, with the acres of overgrown red clover and alfalfa fields and orchards everywhere that attract bears, mile after mile of new-fledged wilderness that has not been bulldozed because a strip through the middle of it is slated to become a superhighway. Tuffy, Doyle's strike dog, trotted ahead, urinating repeatedly as he warmed to the occasion. He was butter-footed in the beginning, as stiff as if he were walking on ice, having hunted in Holland, Vt., the day before and treed a year-ling, which the hosts and landowners there shot. He has grasshopper legs, a long gazelle waist and a broad face for a dog, providing plenty of space for his teeth and for his smelling-chambers. He's even blacker than a bear, and doesn't lope or pace the way a wolf does, for instance; his gait is gimpier, pointier, pumpier, dancier; his legs seem to dangle—long girlish legs—and there's a trotting-horse quality to him—he has a thin tail and shaky, mule-jigging legs. His ears flop incongruously, like a cartoon puppy's, and yet he sniffed like a jackhammer as he started hunting more smoothly, after relieving his bowels and getting the excess of high spirits out of his system. The stark, gaunt persona of a working dog, whether a sled, hound or attack dog, emerged—the scarred face flattening like a janissary's, the eyes going gaily daft. His tail swung with the degree of interest the smells he encountered aroused. Checking the sides of the road, he knew that we were after bear, not the raccoons of August, when he had first been exercised, and so he only honored raccoon sign with a moment or two. When he found a bobcat's trail he "opened up," as the saying is, his voice falsetto when he first used it, but Doyle went into the woods and led him back.

The chokecherry bushes along our course were fully fruited, and we found clumps where a bear must have rummaged, stripping leaves off the branches and treading down the surrounding brush. But this was action of a week before, there was no scent for Tuffy, and although we generals could see the score, the soldiers who would have to fix on the bear and fight him for us had nothing to go on. We poked around an old millrace and an old house site, where a porcupine as round as a turtle was lurking down among the salty timbers. We looked into a pond, looked at the crumpled barns and farm layouts— eighteen abandoned farms, they said. It was all lovely and elegiac—the farms where nobody lived any more and the dense second-growth wilderness which eventually would be leveled again for the highway.

A heavy dew had made scenting ideal but there was no

bear scent. We drove over to Barton Mountain in the next town, and leaving the dogs in their boxes, searched for some traces of bear in another neglected orchard grown up with spruce and scrub maple, a place where once in a long while a bear is seen in the daylight sitting on its ample rump and raking apples up: maybe a farm boy will sneak close and shoot at it, pulling the gun off-target at the last instant for fear of angering it. Doyle says these current farm kids are losing their touch. He was out helping a family tap sugar trees last March, and keeping quiet about it, saw the boys drilling holes in ashes, lindens, oaks. They tapped any tree that wasn't a spruce. When he himself was young he and his brother would go looking for honeybee trees in the summer. The technique was to take a cigar box, substitute a piece of glass for the sliding wooden top, and put sugar water scented with anise oil inside. Then they would pinch a few bees off the flowers and put them in. The bees, loading up, flew home and brought back others, and quickly more. At intervals he and his brother moved the box fifty or a hundred feet closer to the hive, judging by the direction that the bees were flying. If they moved it too fast they'd lose their bees, so it was a two-day project, until finally the entire hive was shuttling back and forth from the cigar box. One time they traced a swarm for several miles to a grizzled hollow maple tree on the top of a bald hill. They left it intact until the winter, when the bees would be in hibernation, then went with a crosscut saw and cut the tree down, but they discovered that in the meantime mice had moved in and eaten all the loot—the honey and the combs, even the bees.

Doyle walked ahead of me, conversing softly, hardly audible. He talked about "pushing a snowshoe," the treks he makes in the winter. We found a deer skeleton, well picked and scattered, and loads of deer droppings, which although pellety ordinarily, soften up in September when the deer eat apples. No bear turds, however. Doyle and Bob Cody and Eric, each casing a different hillside, got on their walkie-talkies and used up some of their nervous energy. We had started out at six o'clock and it was ten by now, so there were pleasure airplanes in the air, a helicopter, and chain saws going, and truck traffic just below us. The radio itself was jammed with conversations, two or three on every channel: French Canadians, people down in Connecticut gossiping, and even some drawlers from Houston, Texas, brought in by the "skip" phenomenon. Eric told Doyle that he ought to change his rabbit's foot to a side pocket if he wanted his luck to change, Doyle prognosticated on where the bears might be hiding, and simultaneously on the radio channel two boatmen on Long Island Sound were advising one another about what sails they ought to use.

We went over to a ridge on May Mountain where Doyle had farmed until recently and which he hopes to develop as summer real estate, with lawns and artificial lakes. Bob Cody came across a smudged bear print beside a stream, too old for Tuffy to get going on, but since the stream chattered appealingly, we had lunch, let Eric's

49

son, who had been cooped up in the jeep, climb some rocks and stretch his legs, and freed the dogs from their boxes to drink. Bob seemed to grow beefier and more phlegmatic as the heat increased and as our schemes were disappointed. Eric became less adenoidal and adolescent, more like somebody's husband, more grown-up, agreeable and witty. Old man Doyle, whose hair is gray, was wearing his farmer's chore-face—lumpy and tough, his big jaw masticating gum, his eyes narrowed and inaccessible. It was a first lieutenant's face (though he has never been in the service), and a face such as full-time big-game guides wear. His enthusiasm for hunting developed late; if it had seized him as a youngster he might have gone out West to where the wildlife was still large. He trapped bears before he hunted them—this while he was milking cows for a living—baiting them with spoiled fruit in a ravine. The first he caught was a three-legged bear which lay low when he came to check the trap—he was also patrolling his electric fence for a branch that was grounding the wire. He wouldn't have noticed he had a bear except that the trees were peeled completely white for yards around, where it had suffered. Bear traps, teethed medievally, are the cruelest of tools. Eventually Vermont outlawed them, but before that Doyle and many another farmer had stored theirs away in souvenir status, after a private discovery.

Doyle still carries a slingshot to sting bears with but used to be rougher on those that bayed than he is now. If nobody along wanted a trophy, he used to put the animal through an ordeal of three or four hours anyway, running it up a tree and forcing it down to the ground again, he and the gang of kids with him firing bullets into the trunk next to its head. It would have to fight the dogs for the movie cameras, and "tree," then scramble down and "tree" yet again, being hit with stones in its rear end all the while, and run for its life as a finale. If it injured a dog or if anything in the scenario went wrong, of course it was a dead bear. He sold a few bears that he shot to unsuccessful hunters from the city. But all that was in the savagery of his thirties. Now he lets the animal off with a warning if no one along "needs a bear," as he puts it—that is, someone who hasn't already at some point shot a bear. And sometimes he reminisces sympathetically about how the whole world must have seemed to fall in on a bear he caught last week, being chased so far and suddenly finding itself surrounded by more dogs and human beings than it had seen in a lifetime.

Almost every young man needs to bathe in blood at least once, if only his own. The problem is that nobody else can do it for him beforehand and there are many more young men than bears nowadays; automobile accidents take the place of bears. Bear is a big word; Doyle uses it as much as he can; it makes for a better hunt. By now he's such an old hand that he orchestrates the hunts, overseeing the sequence of excitements as well as the hounds and the bear. In preparation for our next trip he'd checked all week for tracks as he drove from town to town making his rounds, and the next Saturday we went out to Brownington Pond and let Tuffy loose in the labyrinthine cedar swamp which stretches behind it.

Tuffy peed on fifteen trees, and so did we, and Doyle and the two younger hunters, as part of the gearing-up process, imprinted bears' feet in the mud by thrusting their bunched knuckles in to represent the toes. (In contrast to the black bears, a grizzly has claw tips marked way out in front, which you may miss at first, like a delayed explosion.)

The chokecherry bushes were stripped and trampled, the thorn apples, crab apples and cranberries had been sampled, and there were scatterings of real tracks too, scuffed and undiagrammatic. Tuffy mouthed a dried bear stool aggressively. Though he is tarpaulin-black, his two partners, Jeff and Zeke, are a pretty brindled brown, with reddish eyes, Jeff ash-faced. Weighing sixty pounds, they stand thigh-high to a man and, like Tuffy, have a fanatic, glassy, vacuous look, a hysteric look, like slaves from the world of Buck Rogers. They were rattling their tails against the panels of the truck, whimpering to go, fighting each other in their impatience. Jeff is the fastest dog—if he jumps a bear he can get half a mile ahead of the pack, although he hasn't quite as fine a voice or nose as Tuffy. Zeke ranks as the second most useful dog because his nose is best, but he is not as tough or bear-minded as Tuff; he'll tie himself up trailing a coon. Tuffy is worth maybe $400 and was bought from a famous string of dogs in Olympia, Washington, that destroys a hundred or more bears a year in some of the seed-woods of Weyerhauser.

This second hunt turned into the classic variety. As it grew plain that at last they all were going to be given something to do, the crated dogs howled pathetically to be let loose. Tuffy had struck a fresh track, voicing the news with abrupt, hornlike barks in monotone at fifteen-second intervals. Guessing that it might be a sow bear with cubs who would only circle within a mile or two when she was pursued, Doyle released Zeke to help Tuffy, thinking he'd put in the other dogs later. But the bear, a young male, streaked straight to the east instead, through the township of Brownington toward Charleston, territory which no doubt was familiar to him from his nightly meanderings. With Zeke and Tuffy ragging him, he followed a series of nearly impenetrable swamps that Doyle calls Bear Alley and that connect in a seven-mile rectangle bordered by hard-top roads and other barriers. Neil, Eric's little son, had been left in the truck with the main radio, and he saw the top of the bear's head rushing through the grass, aiming for a sag between ridges of high land, with both dogs hard after him. Since Neil couldn't manage to operate the radio, however, we tramped through tamarack, cedar and pine, jumping brooks and stumbling through the muddy sloughs, because in order to hunt bear on foot you really have to outbear the bear—go where he goes. The red shirts with buckskin vests looked like a combat uniform, and the men in them slogged about in confusion and listened painfully.

At last, hearing the dogs' mournful-sounding, hectic barks above us in the cut on the ridge, we ran for the three vehicles to try to head the creature off at one of the old logging roads which intersect Bear Alley. A bear's a beast, but once he has been treed and let go he will tree the more readily on the next hunt because of the experience. It doesn't induce him to become fiercer; like the dogs, he is being trained for the later time when you decide to kill him. The bears fare best who take a risk, such as swimming a lake or plunging through a populated area where the dogs are seduced and bewildered. Otherwise the bear had better simply stay on the ground and battle grimly, taking the gumption out of each hound individually, until they drift home one by one and he is left in silence to go his way. Of course for the bear the paradox is that such a truculent nature will get him into trouble in other situations in a settled region like New England, and furthermore he doesn't know until late in the game that the dogs after him aren't just an unusually pertinacious gang of farm collies and are being followed by hunters.

The radios were more than playthings now, as Bob and Eric checked separate hills and ridges in the jeeps, listening for the barking. They kidded Doyle about his age, asking if he was panting from floundering in the swamp, but it was like a group of military scouts putting together information. Finally we all raced for a notable big pine on the crossroad that severs Bear Alley from farmland and from higher open ground at its east end. Sure enough, just as we got there we heard Tuffy and Zeke arrive, hectoring the bear in the tangle of brush and trees. The bear stayed out of sight, so Doyle let loose Jeff, who was frantic, and Bob added his two mature dogs, Belle and Duke, and Eric his two pups. We could hear the ki-yiing when the bear clipped somebody; with so many in the fight he didn't have time to take hold and chew. Smelling us, he didn't come in our direction, and as soon as we moved toward the sounds of scrapping, he started right back toward Brownington Pond again, since there were no rough mountains at hand for him to turn into. "He won't stop to eat cherries!" Doyle shouted, laughing. He said the dogs don't know enough to stop and listen for each other, they only hear their own yelping, but now that they were in a tight pack none of them was going to lose its bearings.

Paralleling the swamp, swinging into it from time to time on the gridwork of lumbering roads, we could interpret the noises of the chase and see tracks spattered here and there. It was a summery weekend morning like the last one, so all around us other recreational activities were under way: people playing badminton and gardening, private planes cruising above us. The bear treed about quarter to ten, after some final sparring, having run five miles on this, his second lap. He was in a jungly patch of marsh next to a pasture filled with Holsteins and junk autos. The cows seemed to be curious more than upset.

We got the farmer's permission to drive as close as we could. Doyle put some bullets in his revolver in case of an emergency; cameras and rifles were unlimbered too. The bear was seventy feet off the ground in the crotch of a tall poplar, the only impressive tree around. A woodpecker was pecking a rotted spar nearby, and the bear himself, perhaps because he was so high, apparently did not recognize that this was a life-and-death meeting, or else he was maintaining his dignity. He seemed as removed from our mundane glory-whoops and the dogs' inane tromboning as a bear in a zoo; or maybe every wild animal by now has come to look like an animal in a zoo. He twitched his nose, lifted his head to see if there wasn't a branch higher still, and opened his mouth a little, like a gorilla yawning, playing it close to the vest, not wanting to draw attention to himself in case we were ready to go away. He licked his paws for the moisture on them, because he must have been very thirsty. He was resting. Doyle guessed that he was three or four years old and weighed upwards of two hundred pounds, though he was a bit thin. He had large, lengthy arms, a handsome, straight substantial head, and did not appear panicky, just uncomfortable and uneasy. In the beginning he pushed his tongue out of his mouth because he was thirsty and hot, but later he did it as a signal of pugnacity, looking down at the dogs and tilting his head slightly, as if he didn't wish to show us he was looking down. Animals are alert to note where another animal is looking, and many of them—from bighorn sheep to wolves—scrape their tongues in and out between their teeth to indicate a willingness to fight.

Throughout, Bob Cody shrieked and yelled, at a pitch; Eric crowed and thumped the tree trunk with a post. They encouraged the dogs to yelp and leap as high against the tree as a man could have, and they excited them so much that Duke and Jeff began to tussle uproariously. The bear was so high up that I had to walk away a hundred feet to see him. He leaned back on his rump above us, looking at the tops of other trees and at the branches of the pop-

lar above him, as if for an avenue higher and higher. As
he became increasingly unhappy, he moved his gray
muzzle in confidential ruminations like a traveler who
finds that the traveling companions with whom he's penned
are in fact renegades. Eventually, while the dogs were
being disciplined and the cameras were clicking, while
we were festively busy at the base of the tree, he began
coming down. Altogether he'd had nearly an hour's rest.
His long, relaxed, powerful, gorilla-type arms grasping
the trunk slung him upwards or downwards or around the
tree with very little effort.

Much hollering on our part; guns were grabbed again.
He paused halfway down, hanging in place like a
telephone lineman and watching us and looking off. His
life hung in the balance, although he didn't know that.
The hunters really didn't know that his life hung in the
balance either; they knew they'd shoot him to save the
dogs but they didn't really comprehend that he'd be dead.
Which is the trouble with most hunters, and why when
one of them shoots another, the shooter generally col-
lapses, vomits, has to have his rifle taken away immediately, has to have his remaining companions sleep beside
him, hold and comfort and reassure and protect him,
even keep him from doing violence to himself. Suddenly
the man realizes that he has been dealing with the miracle
of death.

But after considering, the bear climbed back up. Doyle
cut a twig for a toothpick and told the dogs, "You beat
the son-of-a-gun! That's all we wanted." Between the
dogs' baying, the Choctaw yells, Bob's banging a pole

against the tree for the last footage in the camera, there was a terrific racket. I noticed that although I couldn't smell the bear himself, I could smell uprooted grass and bark torn off the tree. He was extremely discomposed by now, stirring up there. After ten more minutes, he came almost all the way down, making no fuss when he started, just swinging down feet first in silence, with his long forearms clutching the trunk, his vigorous body like some ancestral figure's. He seemed to be hoping that we were prepared to call it a day if he simply came down, uncontentious, nonchalant. It's hard to keep a good bear up a tree, as Doyle had said, but we didn't give in to him and he hung overhead for a long while, chopping his jaws softly and snarling—a fluffing, breathy sound. Then he climbed clear up again. The noble dimensions of the tree and the bear's moxie were making it a perfect treeing.

Since the cameras were empty and this was only supposed to be an exercise, Doyle and the others caught their dogs. Immediately, even before they'd leashed them, the bear came skidding down, hasty as a fireman. When he was six feet from the ground he leaped straight out for cover. One of the hounds got loose, unfortunately, so that they all had to be released so the single dog would not come to grief. They ran the bear for two or three more miles, back east toward Charleston and the big pine. Eric and Bob in the two jeeps, knowledgeably speeding around to an intersection, contrived to meet the bear just as he emerged in a clearing. Letting him go by, they intercepted the dogs while he was still tiredly breaking brush within their hearing.

"Tuffy seems to be lost, Paul!" they told Doyle when we reached them, because kidding the latecomer is traditional in hunting.

A week later, we attempted somewhat wistfully to re-capitulate these triumphs by taking the dogs to Brown-ington swamp at dawn again. Lakes of fog lay between the hills; frost tufted the goldenrod, the fields of hard-hack and the evergreens. We listened to a farm boy shouting at cows in the distance. Doyle once ran a herd-testing station, and as we dawdled by the truck, feeling that this repeat performance would never equal the last time, he talked about the sidelines that a farmer has, like trucking Christmas trees to New York City in the frantic weeks before Christmas, or cutting his cedar woods to sell to the fence-post factory. Then the sugar bush—a hillock of maple trees—which could take maybe four thousand taps if you wanted to kill yourself but which you tap with one thousand, feeling overworked at that—and finally have the hill logged off for cash. Lately, most farmers plan for the profits involved in real estate. Doyle says that even Bear Alley has been changing hands. He himself has acquired a real estate agent's license to complement his insurance business; yet on these hunts he's such an obvious woodsman, such a chunk-jawed, rugged deadeye, that one has the impression of a vocation lost.

The scenting conditions were ideal: no rain to wash the traces away but a dousing of dew to spice and accentuate whatever there was. We led the dogs on leashes into the brush to get a fast jump on the bear if Tuffy, who was out ahead, found one. Bloodhounds have the best noses of any dog, but they are slow and not aggressive, and they walk on their ears when their heads are down. Slogging through the mud, the streams and over deadfalls, we saw an osprey's nest and paths of coons and porcupines. Deep in the swamp there was a tin shanty where several lumberjacks had lived. There was plenty of bear sign too, though nothing recent. Tuffy was puzzling along an unproductive trail; we listened to him respectfully, wading in tangents whenever he turned. We climbed a sunny knoll and waited. He was on a beechnut ridge to the south, croaking like a chicken; then he entered a sugar orchard. Eric and Bob went off to listening posts on crowns of hills around the countryside, so there was lots of compass-reading and horsing with the radios. "The needle in the haystack," said Doyle. Once he killed a wild boar that had wandered into this part of the state from a private game preserve. "He was all shoulders when we saw him run, so we knew that if he wasn't a wild boar he must be a buffalo."

The French Canadians came on the radio again, speaking a French like leaden Spanish, and half a dozen Americans. The chain saws were starting up like motorboats. Getting tired of waiting for Tuffy to strike something, we drove around to a crossroads and caught him. We drove to the town of Westmore, checking in various orchards, finding deer beds and bushes that the bucks had stripped when rubbing velvet off their antlers. At midmorning we went to look at a cow carcass which a woman had buried a week before, using her tractor, and which she said a bear was digging up. Unlike so many tips, however, her report turned out to be true. The evidence of digging and chewing at the black remains was plain; also the tack which he had taken through a hemlock woods towards the hiding place where he lay up during the day. Spirits surged, and though the scent was dry, for his sins we tramped round and about for another hour or two with all due military drama, generating in ourselves the sensation that the war in the woods hadn't actually been won a century ago, that we were needed, that this bear exhuming the week-old carcass of a cow was a real emergency.

"Look out, now. There's a black dog loose. I don't want you jumping out of your skin thinking he's a bear, if he comes up behind you," Doyle kidded Cody.

We drove back to the notable white pine at the end of Bear Alley, where we had listened to the dogs ki-yiing in the screen of trees. It wasn't far; and here too we found tracks—faint, hand-sized imprints in the road, like Sanskrit underlying the language of the many tire and boot marks. This may have been the bear whose endeavors we had just been inspecting at the cow's grave, or even the same bear we had treed in the poplar tree the week before. He had to eat something, and bears aren't overly plentiful today. Necessarily, there will be more and more of this business of letting the bear go after treeing him; bears will be run up a tree quite regularly; it will be like a kind of bear-baiting. Bears may become one of the group of animals whose welfare will be associated with the paper industry, since they hide out in the pulp woods. I think that Doyle probably would spare all those his dogs tree except that earning the $100 guiding fee pleases him. It's not the sum of money, which doesn't seem as much to a busy insurance agent as it might to a man who was still milking cows for a living, but rather the role in which he earns it: professionally guiding hunters. A hundred dollars is little enough to pay for a bear in the 1970s, and enormous numbers of hunters in Massachusetts and New York are eager to pay it. Sight unseen, they call him up and say flatly that if he can find them a bear—if he knows where one is living—they will be up in four hours, right then and there, any time, any day. It puts him in a quandary.

I stopped at the taxidermist's next day. By coincidence, a bear had just been brought in, lying in a pickup truck. It had been shot in Franconia, New Hampshire, and was a male of seven or eight, weighing perhaps three hundred pounds. The hunter, a wiry long-haired man from Florida, was inside the shop consulting about prices. He had a sharp and knowing tipster's face, clever and gay. His wife had come along for the ride. She was pregnant and pleasant-looking, wearing white lipstick, her hair rinsed a white-blond. He was as short as she, and they appeared to have achieved the marriage-of-friends that most of us seem to be heading for. The bear lay on its back, its legs extended upwards, each one bent differently, so that its posture was like a man lying *in extremis* next to the site of a catastrophe. In height it might have compared to a fourteen-year-old boy, but it was built like a barrel. After its head had been sawn off, what remained looked like a prisoner must look after visiting the guillotine, a circle of vital red stuff jamming its neck. It looked truncated and shortened and uncompleted, like an uncolored figure in a coloring book. The paws also were cut off to be mounted and all the rest of the bear, in its ragged September coat, was thrown away. After asking whether they ought to cut off "steaks," the Floridians tooled out of town in search of a covert where they could dispose of the trunk and legs. They were flirting and celebrating because, as the fellow said, this was a big event. Thousands and thousands of guys are out in the woods and in a lifetime of hunting you may only manage to see one bear.

THE ELEPHANT
TRAINER AND THE
MAN ON STILTS

Catch the circus this spring [1969], if you are the type who thinks of going but then generally doesn't; it's the best version of the circus we have had for at least ten years. Ringling Bros. and Barnum & Bailey is still "the Big One" in the circus business, for better or worse, but John Ringling North sold the show recently, and so the music, for instance, has been immensely improved by the simple fact that the band is allowed to play music composed by professionals now, instead of music composed by John Ringling North. The conductor, Merle Evans, is old to be doing two or three shows a day, but they've given him back his brass section at last instead of a nightclub-Disneyland score, and if you're an aficionado, you can close your eyes and watch the whole show in your mind's eye, hearing him play. The elephants and the tigers have been trained by a young trainer from Germany named Gunther Gebel-Williams, who is probably the best all-around animal man to come

to America for twenty years. First he works alone with his
cats, as lithe and on top of things as Clyde Beatty once
was, but with a gentle, fertile, inventive delight, a sinful,
delicious intimacy, and frank joy—he works like a genius,
in other words. He has a Fighter, a Stealthy One, and a
Hatstand, eight altogether. He gives them the "How"
salute of an animal man to a tiger, hand raised and palm
flat, and bats them with the butt end of his whip to keep
them slinking and roaring, nonplussed. He could go on
playing with them forever, blending and understating
his feats, but all pleasures must end; the fourteen elephants come on and he gives these a run for their money
as well, with a Peter Pan grin, a crucifix bouncing on his
bare chest. In his slippers, he rollerskates on their backs.
The usual elephant handler we see in this country is a
rocko-socko Arkansan about fifty-five, assisted by numerous husky drunks and jailbirds, one assigned to each
creature to supervise every move that it makes—there are
tremendous groans from the beasts and lots of whaling
and whacking with sticks. This fellow treats them like
mothers or sisters, however, or maybe like overgrown
tigers. He leaves leeway for their bashful grace, does
practically all the directing with his voice alone, and runs
and runs and runs like the wind in order to be everywhere
at once. Circus music is really music to run to and walk
to—to walk to the high wire with and finish and walk
away with: a sort of a walk through life.

Most of the other staple acts are also first-rate. Two
flying trapeze troupes bring off that delicate acrobatic
coup, the triple, which is rarely seen and which Burt

Lancaster practiced so earnestly to perfect in the movie *Trapeze*. A man clowns on the high wire with the cut mouth, stark nose and hollow yells which are the hallmarks of all of us in time of woe. There are teeterboard tumblers who manage to flip themselves four-high; a man stunts on a lofty sway-pole; a pretty girl does tricks with swords and wineglasses on a tall ladder; some unicyclists play flashy basketball; and Victoria Unus wrenches herself around and around in a vertical circle at the end of a rope some seventy times, a particularly arduous act that is seldom performed. There is Roman riding with Indian yells. Someone hangs from a trapeze bar by his toes while the crowd sighs with relish. The women still look like Sonja Henie, they wear fountains of feathers, and the men have strong jaws. The rigging is something between a stupendous erector set and a nervous breakdown, and the spotlights turn the air milky and pink. The timing is tight and the bill of fare lavish, with the three rings New Yorkers have come to expect. (Three rings is nice for the grownups, of course, but sometimes bewilders young children. Unless Ringling Bros. is exceptionally fine, as it is this year, children may do better at the Moscow Circus when it is in town, a more chummy, closely knit show with obvious *esprit.*)

I was glad not to see many jugglers, magicians, or chimp acts, pony acts and other small sufferers—these being interludes I usually yawn through. Chimp trainers look like failed dancing-school teachers. But the circus has sustained a severe loss in regard to its clowns. Some of the great ones retired; some went into television, pricing themselves out of the business; and one famous clown was murdered last year. Because most performers are Europeans from circus families, we keep getting stunning new talent executing the austere and ancient physical feats, but clowning has been the one American fief—clowning of the kind that we like, at least. Youngsters who ran away from home to join the circus were already too old to learn the more precise crafts of the show but they could become clowns; now, in a changing world, they don't join the circus when they run away and they don't become clowns. Like the rodeo, and like boxing, the circus predates our familiar team sports, such as football or baseball. Like them, it's a splash of bodily virtuosity carried over from another era, and it has the same primitive grandeur they do—except we don't tend to feel so uncomfortable with it, don't find it unduly uncouth and brutal. Unfortunately, we just aren't as interested any more, either. Only the performers are interested, and without much public encouragement they train and prepare and carry on.

Ringling Bros. and Barnum & Bailey had its heyday in the years from the First World War to the Wall Street crash. Forty elephants were performing then, and llamas, camels, zebras and gnus strolled in the "spec," with as many as forty-eight lions and tigers in Clyde Beatty's cage. The Depression, the Second World War, the calamitous Hartford circus fire in 1944, the dilettantism of the North management, and the onslaught of television all dealt the big vulnerable show a series of blows which culminated in the owner's decision in 1956 to fold the tents and play only extended engagements indoors. Once it was done, this was irrevocable, and for someone like me, anyway, who had worked in the circus in the early fifties, the spellbinding elements of the scene had not been so much the performance itself but the billowing big top, the constant hustle of tearing it down and putting it up again, the nightly hop to a new cornfield, and all the paraphernalia of wagons and trucks. A number of old-time circus people left Ringling Bros. to join the few little circuses that were still under canvas, and my own reaction, when I started going to the show as a paying customer, was to sit way high up in the cheapest seats where I could hear the band well and watch the whole spectacle but not see anything terribly close. I let my memories wash through me and picked the good ones. Even so, it generally made for a sad evening.

But this year the downward drift has been stopped; nothing is perfunctory. And from Frankie Saluto to Harold Ronk, the circus hands revel at the reprieve. It's a youthful and cheerful show. The accountants are out to save money, but they're saving it in the right ways, doing without the sideshow, for instance, always an eyesore, and doing without the static tableaux floats. The ballet girls are still beautiful, and riding the elephants throws their breasts around. The elephants are masked like raccoons because they spray water on their own eyes. They toot through their trunks in a clarinet key. And there is a purposeful man on stilts. He's the last man to leave, striding out of the hippodrome at the end of the show with a swift but laborious gait, like some handicapped, brilliantly gifted personage who is silent after the hoopla. When he has disappeared, the rings stand empty and one is left lonely.

THE CIRCUS CONTD. (1970)

Anniversaries in the circus world tend to serve as occasions for ballyhoo, and sometimes are invented for that purpose. The claim that this particular year is Ringling Bros. and Barnum & Bailey's 100th Anniversary is backed up by a story too complicated to attempt to tell. Nevertheless, the circus right now is in good hands, and rainbow-rococo anachronism though it is, is attempting a renaissance. It deserves every possible edge. It has divided one huge, basic show into two units in order to appear in different cities simultaneously. What reaches New York, naturally, is the best foot it can put forward. The individual acts in this centennial version are not better than last year's and there aren't any more of them, but the staging is perhaps trimmer, the stop-go choreography tighter, and the relay-race momentum more assured. The surviving elephant herd is presented under the direction of Hugo Schmitt, an old-timer from tenting days, and they go through such contortions that we see even their poignant dugs. There is a strutting hubbub in the rings: cowgirls, redskins and giraffe-necked women, dirndls,

69

Balkan-Andalusian costumes, men who would as soon be standing on their hands as on their feet, and a setter-sized burro, fat-assed horses with pyramids of people on them, and waltzing horses and long whips. The dome of the Garden becomes an echo chamber, the air is full of hanging rigging and of people, chartreuse and magenta lighting. Tom Thumb swings his cane. P. T. Barnum and Jenny Lind clop by in a carriage. Emanuel Zacchini is shot out of a cannon. Fattini on his sway-pole puffs smoke so vigorously that we begin to worry most about his lungs; then, wrapping his legs around the pole, he slides down head first towards the blinding floodlight. There are teeterboards and cushiony tumblers, and smiling dogs with smiling ladies, a headdressed stunt girl on a white ball, a raw big bear trainer driving six frightened bears through rudimentary chores.

The great contemporary animal trainer is Gunther Gebel-Williams, who presently is traveling with Ringling Bros.' other unit, the so-called red show (this being the "blue"). Charly Baumann handles the tigers here. He's a cool, good-hearted, hulking fellow, neither brilliant nor inspired; but he likes the work. He's relaxed and rather dawdling and friendly with the cats, makes the hard look easy, and does not travesty or humiliate them, just exhibits their elegance, their lovely coats. With little fuss and clatter—no snarls, just a few pleasantly resonant, drumlike roars—he keeps them reaching upwards for the point of his whip or doing gentle stunts. One friend of his, a sort of St. Francis among tigers, mouths and hugs him several times, and later rides a horse and plays with a blond girl named Evy. During the previous act, in the darkness of the cage, Baumann can be seen checking on his friend's frame of mind, playing pawsie and bestowing kisses, both American and Eskimo—really a more endearing moment than after the lights go on. He has eleven tigers. Since there are less than one-fifteenth as many tigers left on the Indo-Pakistan subcontinent as there were in the 1920s, these in captivity represent a gaudy remnant who are living their last days. Now, with the decimation of the animal kingdom all around the world (there are seven hundred rhinoceroses left), we are shown only "highlights" of what we used to see. The big cage in the center ring used to contain a cornucopia of heavy-weight maned lions, and welterweight leopards as quick as pistons, and hissing, buckskin-colored pumas, a few mute, miming polar bears, maybe a dumbhead jaguar or two, an orange contingent of tigers, and even a subdued Great Dane.

Bill Ballantine has done a good job with the clowns this year, rebuilding a shattered corps. One clown wears a sweater that is thirty yards long. The Gaona family are the latest in a great progression of Mexican trapeze stars. The equestrian Althoffs and the Poldi family of acrobats also are fine; and the Brizios do a Chaplin slapstick act with housepaint, flipping it around, at last hauling off and socking one another. Elvin Bale, son of a trouping tiger trainer of two decades ago, seems to be the stars' star of the show. More than anybody else, he risks his neck, doing a series of splendid heel catches on the single-trapeze, making them look awfully easy, with the face and the elation of a young Lindbergh.

I wished for a high-wire-walking act, because that is traditional and generally crowns a show. I wished for a slack-wire act, because dancing on the slack wire is an ancient, neglected skill. I wished that there were tanbark on the floor instead of sheets of canvas, and wished the band music (after Merle Evans' retirement) weren't turning toward being mere blues or ordinary convention music, supplanting those old vinegary, elided marches— the high cornets and sumptuous cymbals and unabashed trombones and tubas which are the legs and buttocks of the show. "Quality Plus" and "World Events" and "Entry of the Gladiators" ought to be played. "The Crimson Petal"; "Royal Bridesmaids"; "Pageant of Progress"; "March Ponderoso"; "Colossus of Columbia"; and "Bull Trombone."

But these are quibbles of a lover. I liked the stylish curtsies and the command-performance bows, the prov-ing-of-the-feat where swords were used. The truth is that the circus offers the best three hours that are for sale in the United States. Now that the arts on which it is founded are declining in Western Europe as well as here, the Ringling management has journeyed to East Europe to sign the best that can be had. The night I watched, the audience was thin and dim and slow to clap, the timing of several key acts was off, and finally a trapezist fell and broke his arm. But then Zacchini, who had been out of action since January after an accident in Jacksonville, was shot from his cannon, sailed grandly through the air, and landed safe and sound, swung himself out of the net, and ran to the performers' entrance, and kissed a young woman who was waiting for him in a wheelchair streaming tears. Zacchini's father, a circus stalwart, first shot himself from a cannon in 1929; so it was another beginning.

KNIGHTS AND SQUIRES:
FOR LOVE OF
THE TUGS

The greatest sightseeing jaunt in New York City is to cross Brooklyn Bridge on the footway, which is raised above the vehicular traffic, a relic of the day when pedestrians were thought to be gentlemen and had at least equal footing with horses and buggies. The bridge is constructed of beautiful sandstone pillars, gothically arched, and cables which cross one another as in a fish net but which are engineered into gigantic parallel harps. "I love you, Hart Crane!" somebody has written up there, and it is kingly, it's like skywalking, with the architecture of a couple of centuries crammed into the enclave of downtown Manhattan, and the harbor out past Governor's Island glinting like platinum when the sun is right. If you like beaches, maybe the pleasantest beach within the city is South Beach on Staten Island, bordering the Narrows. Take the ferry— the floating hatbox—and a No. 2 bus. The small-town reliefs and relaxants of Staten Island are finally disappearing and we have in their place Verrazano Bridge, with a long, low, regal trajectory, as splendid and cool as mathematics is.

But by early summer I, for one, become something of a menace to myself. Spring fever isn't the word for it; I want to get to the country. Impatiently, I don't bother looking for cars when I cross the street, my favorite parks hardly hold me, and while these great bridges, triumphs of tension and engineering, and the real pitch pipes of a maritime city, boost me out of the banging streets for a minute, they make me squint because they perform a balancing act I can't perform—that kinetic balancing. Eventually, what I do is to call up the Moran tugboat company and ask to go out on one of their boats for the day. They're Irish believers in brotherhood, and year after year they benignly agree.

Moran, which is an old paternal firm closely involved in New York harbor politics, has been pressed by its competition lately and its personnel no longer effuse quite the confident air of a local navy. But compared to the other freeholders of the life of the city, the tugs have kept a remarkable independence. A Huck Finn type wouldn't feel any more crowded on board now than in the days before the invention of radios when the boats sold water and chandlers' stores and waited outside the Narrows to bargain with every ship's captain as to what he would pay to be escorted in. ("Big storm comin'!") When you watch from the shore, the boatmen pop in and out of hatches and cause visual tricks in moving around. If they walk forward they accentuate the rush of the tug and look to be wearing Bunyan boots, whereas, going aft, they are a study in conflicting motions, striding so fast yet apparently standing still. And when you see a tug steam down the North River against the backdrop of the Palisades—it's a wide Adirondack river smelling of fir forests and mountain streams poured together (among other things)—the rustic tug coasts down like a square trader's raft, painted rough colors and draped with those pelty hemp fenders that look as brown and chop-edged and sloppy and wild as so many beaver furs or big bear-skins.

Moran boats are barn-red with black stacks exhibiting a prominent white M. They deal with most of the ocean-going ships and do a good part of the other work of the harbor as well—pushing the garbage, fuel and traprock barges, sand scows, lighters, dredges, coal buckets. Moran operates towboats down the Atlantic seaboard to New Orleans, Bermuda and Puerto Rico, and in the Erie Canal; here in New York they have twenty to thirty boats working. Each one is a corporation, to limit lawsuit liability, and each is crewed by three men for a shift, besides a cook. Some are round-the-clock boats and some are "day boats," which go out in the morning and come in at night, with long but varied hours according to the work scheduled. For a twelve-hour day a captain's base pay is around $75 and a deckhand's perhaps $50. A captain who handles shipping, however, is also a docking pilot, earning a separate fee for each ship that he docks. The fee is determined by the ship's length ($10 per 100

76

feet) and goes into a pool with all the fees other docking pilots in the harbor have earned, to be divvied up at the end of the month like the spoils of a World Series team. Though there are half and quarter shares, experienced pilots may make $40,000 a year. "I don't even let myself think about it," says the public relations man.

Ten years ago I was reading the *Journal American* in tugboat galleys, and five years ago the *Daily Mirror,* and recently I went to the Battery again and was led aboard the *Teresa Moran,* a new, 4290-horsepower, round-the-clock boat which had just changed crews, as it does every other day. Captain Biagi was to pilot the *United States* from its slip in the North River at noon. Earlier in the morning, according to the log, the *Teresa* had docked the *Raeffaello* and sailed the tanker *Stolt Falcon.* Biagi's back hurt because he'd been raking fertilizer into his lawn the day before; he's peppy, talkative, competent, clever, and lives in East Brunswick, New Jersey. His co-captain, also licensed as a pilot, was Ray Carella. Carella, who started on the Erie Canal at sixteen as a deckhand, now lives in East Meadow, Long Island, but is a gaunter, less assured, somber man. Throughout the day the two of them shared the piloting jobs so that both would stand well in the pool. The deckhands were Ture Eklund, a soft-spoken, civilized fellow who lives in Westchester County and builds model boats, and Walter Anglim, a raw-boned, rugged American sort. The two engineers were Tom Rasmussen—young, gangly and energetic—and Joe Gallant, a husky, hard-headed old customer; the cook was Candy Coelho, a

Portuguese who is a veteran of forty-four years on the tugs, though his tightly smooth face doesn't show it. He and Biagi and Gallant told stories of the Depression.

The assignments came at two-hour intervals instead of an hour apart, as they often do. We made no extended trips to Newark or Constable Hook or into the Kills, didn't get tangled in Newton Creek, Brooklyn, or spend the day locked into Wallabout Bay. The nearest tug to a job usually gets it, so you can spend a whole shift just in the thickets of Red Hook, emptying slip after slip and filling them up again. The railroads have their own tugs, as do the principal oil companies, but the free-lance tugboats handle the freighters and do the hundreds of queer little noncom jobs in the back corners, hauling copper and newsprint, and stopping along the way as a favor to somebody, to tell the *Gunvor Brovig*, for instance, which is anchored off Rosebank, that a Sandy Hook pilot should be getting to her about four o'clock—her radio's off.

The *United States*, though the biggest of ships, is not a particularly memorable proposition among all the tasks that come to a tug. We were helped by the *Esther Moran*, which tied onto the stem: we were at the bow, with Carella in the wheelhouse. Captain Biagi, on the ship's bridge, gave his directions by walkie-talkie, each tug answering with its peep whistle to confirm that the order was understood. Two longshoremen cast the hawsers off, and the ship, its engines reversed, provided its own motive power, while the *Teresa* and *Esther* kept it clear of the pier. Especially at the Manhattan piers, which are finger wharfs, built at right angles to the river, undocking a ship is a great deal simpler than docking it. The ship has been moored bow-in, so the tug which is at the bow only acts as a rudder as the ship backs away. In a kind of a dance, the *Teresa* nudged first one side of the stem, then the other—the stem looming overhead as sharp as a blade. There were acres of black steel plating, rivets in twisting patterns, and the two anchors like a whale's eyes. The ship blasted its whistle to warn any traffic on the river and in no time it had backed into the current, whereupon the two tugs pushed it around ninety degrees to head towards the sea. Compared to the rigamarole of warping a big ship into its slip, this was easy as kicking your shoes off, though we did have to bustle over to the pier once again, and out to the ship, and then back over to the pier again in a comedy routine because a bevy of voyagers had missed the gangplank and some partying visitors on board the ship had gotten drunk and forgotten to leave.

Afterwards Biagi called 17 Battery Place for the next assignment, and we were sent around Lower Manhattan and up the East River to an oil depot at 138th Street in the East Bronx to sail the Liberian tanker *St. Grigorousa.* I went to the engine room with Rasmussen, who wears earmuffs, and examined the twin diesel engines, the steering mechanism, the air compressors, but I couldn't pay much attention, becoming panic-stricken as I was painfully deafened. However, the cabins are comfortable places, and the wheelhouse has high-legged chairs and lots of windows amidst all the radar equipment and compasses. The radio drawled messages to the other tugs in a comradely fashion: "Seventeen to the *Harriet*"; "Seventeen to the *Eugenia*." A brusque rainy wind blew outside, and the ebb tide boiled spray at our bow. Manhattan is variegated, sway-backed and dumpy as you go by, not composed of monolithic glass towers, and the piers are almost all ramshackle; yet in a way the view is encouraging because from the water New York does not have the appearance of a city destroying itself—there is just too much of it. Even the loss of a specific harborside landmark like the razing of the Fulton Fish Market will scarcely be noticeable from out on the water.

A silent back stretch, 138th Street is beyond Hellgate Bridge, off Sunken Meadows and by North Brothers Island, where the planes sweep low every thirty seconds to land at LaGuardia Airport. The *St. Grigorousa,* scruffy, patch-painted, offered no problems, except that our tug in maneuvering got careless and snapped a few pilings on an adjoining dock. The Greeks on the ship watched this little miscalculation with the attention which seamen of different nationalities bestow on each other's blunders. Anglim had had trouble throwing a line up on deck, and that interested them too. They were unwashed, unsmiling, windblown, and they had a nubile-looking young boy aboard.

A bit past Gracie Mansion, while we were accompanying them downriver, Biagi still piloting on the bridge of the ship, we saw the *Marie Moran,* the *Patricia Moran* and the *Esther* pushing against the broad side of a lumber boat, the *Seamar* from Coos Bay, Oregon, which had managed to draw parallel with its pier but was unable to approach closer. This was at Green Street, in Brooklyn. The radio told us to go to its assistance quickly, the captain of the *St. Grigorousa* gave his permission, and in a moment the Greeks had let our line down. Without waiting for Biagi to come off the ship, we swung away, and putting our bow amidships on the *Seamar,* shoved full ahead for what amounted to nearly an hour. Our extra horsepower did stop the drifting, but then no more progress was made, though the four tugs shifted position and pushed as hard as they could. First the outflowing tide had been the villain, but soon it was just a case of the ship being so heavily loaded that her keel was touching the bottom; we were trying to push her into a list sufficient to bring her deck close to the dock where the cranes would be able to unload her. It was a tedious business; the tug captains talked back and forth on the radio and talked to the pilot, who was from the *Patricia.*

Until recently walkie-talkies weren't used from ship to tug. Instead, the pilot signaled a tugboat at the bow of the ship by blowing codes on an ordinary police whistle. One whistle meant half speed ahead; several shorts, full ahead; two shorts, two shorts meant slow. The tug would repeat the message on its peeper, and then the pilot would signal the tugs at the stern with the ship's own deep-throated, significant whistle, which they promptly answered, all in the same code: so the harbor has lost some of the chatter it had.

Finally we left the *Teresa*'s three sisters shouldering

81

the *Seamar* and headed for Governor's Island to pick up
Biagi, who had been deposited on a small barge boat
called the *Lester,* as we were told. A German freighter,
the *Hilde Mittman,* was traveling beside us as we entered
the curve that the East River makes near Delancey Street.
At the same time, however, a tug called the *Carol Moran*
was coming upriver, as well as a Penn Central Railroad
tug which was roped between two unwieldy carfloats.
The *Hilde* was outside of us and signaled them both to
go outside of her—or, in other words, closer to Brooklyn
—but the *Carol* swerved inside instead, between the
Hilde Mittman and us. The *Hilde* had to veer toward the
railroad tug suddenly, and the railroad tug was almost
forced into a pier on the Brooklyn side of the river—
trying to avoid a collision, she reversed engines and swung
dangerously sideways, and the bow lines on one of the
carfloats broke. The *Carol* went on, the *Hilde* went on,
but we lingered a moment or two to see whether she
needed help.

Our next job, not scheduled till six o'clock, was to help
a McAllister tug sail the freighter *Fraternity,* registered
in Monrovia, from Pier 1 in the Erie Basin. We passed a
good many ships in berths on the way: the *Alamahdi,* the
Concordia Lago, the *Lexa Maersk,* the *Lichtenfels.* A
paint-company launch puttered by, towing rafts and
scaffolding; also a union launch collecting dues from the
barge and the lighter men whom it encountered. The sun
had come out, the weather was warming up genially.
Tugboats ride very low in the water, with the stubby bow
pushing waves that are higher than the decks. It was a

lovely, foamy, noisy trip. Standing on the fantail, I had the sense I was aquaplaning, a feeling of victory. "How are you doing—meditating?" asked Eklund.

Erie Basin is a narrow, rectangular, concrete facility with a narrow hole for an entrance which lies in South Brooklyn not far beyond Buttermilk Channel. There were at least six other ships in there, and one of the captains stepped out in his shirtsleeves on the bridge to lean on the railing and watch the work, in case any sideswiping occurred. McAllister tugs are parvenus that have taken a good deal of business away from Moran lately, so some rather elaborate courtesies ensued between the *Helen McAllister* and us. "At your service, Captain." "Surely, Captain." But we squeezed the *Fraternity* out of its slip and through the hole of the basin without difficulty. Eklund, a relaxed man, worked with brief motions, snuggling the thick Dacron line around the horns of the bitt as easily as if he were tightening his belt. He added coils to snub it fast, funneling the tugboat's power through the stretching rope—which makes a sinister sound like a rattlesnake's rattle—or loosening and changing the coils during the lax interludes when the tug, on instructions, floated at dead stop. Since the foredeck of the tug is short, he worked ten feet inboard, watching not the ship but the rope. And when the tug's rumbling engines announced another session of physics, he tossed several more coils on the bitt, watching them writhe and creak and tighten.

The sailors threw down our line. The McAllister man, who had been the pilot, climbed over the rail and down a ladder, leaving the Sandy Hook pilot in charge. It's always a sharply focused instant when a ship separates from the tugs. Water slashed in as the gap opened; the wind seemed to blow harder, no longer blocked by the ship, and it was an ocean wind. For the first time, the ship's screw kicked up a deep, worldly froth, a green wake, and the *Fraternity* pointed away, leaving us where we were.

There are about a hundred and forty-five Sandy Hook pilots, who guide the ships in and out of New York, from the Sea Buoy off Sandy Hook to the Battery or to the vicinity of the pier. They are paid a fee of $10 per foot of draft by the shipping company, so routinely they may make $250 per ship, but out of that they must pay the expenses of their profession—the pilot boat and crew—and they get no additional salary, such as a docking pilot receives from Moran. As often as not, the Sandy Hook pilot, the tugboat pilot and the ship's master spend their half hour together on the ship's bridge exchanging stock-market tips—at least I've often heard a tug captain come down the ladder and say that's what they'd talked about, complaining because the ship's master only knew about foreign stocks.

We were told to wait awhile in the Gowanus Canal for an eight o'clock job. The cook fed us cube steak and beet salad. Years ago, when I was younger and hungrier, part of my pleasure was the feasts on a tugboat. The cooks buy their own food on an allowance of three dollars a day for each crew member, but the money went further then and the meals were baronial. A first course of herring in wine sauce, honeydew melon, shrimp cocktail, pickles and olives, soup and a choice of juices, all of them served simultaneously. A main course of roast beef, roast lamb, fillet of sole, macaroni and cheese and cold cuts, plus corn, squash, peas, lima beans, two salads, two kinds of potatoes. And there would be pies, rice pudding, a cake, ice cream, brownies, date bread, iced and hot drinks, Camembert cheese, and canned and new fruit. "Goes with the meal. Eat up. That's the best meat right next to the bone," the Norwegian cook used to say, bending over and pointing or pouring gravy, crushing an empty milk carton in his other hand.

Anglim and Eklund took the opportunity to hook a hose to the hydrant there in Gowanus and freshen the water tanks. The *Aqua,* an antique Victorian steam-driven boat that peddles water throughout the harbor, waited her turn alongside. Since the Canal is laughably tortuous and is filled with ships, you can get stuck there working all night. But the *Kerry Moran* was heading our way from Bush Terminal, so she was switched to our post and we were asked to move on across the Upper Bay to Pier F in Jersey City, which faces some of the grass-grown, abandoned piers of Lower Manhattan. En route we stopped like responsible citizens to tie up three Lehigh Valley barges that had broken loose from a dock. We saw a large fire in the Houston Street area, and I wrote down more names of ships that we passed: the *Covadonga,* the *Nordfarer,* the *Baie Comeau,* the *Cap Norte,* the *Todos os Santos,* the *Cyril,* an almanac of the world.

The *Baltic Sea* (Goteborg) was our new eight o'clock

ship. Eklund heaved up the throwing line, which has a ball on the end so that it will hang over the ship's rail until it's retrieved. Since the ship was white, he put a white cloth over our bow, where we would rub paint. Up on deck the silent Swedes with their beards and curly blond hair and muted manner looked down at us, though their captain was pacing restlessly. We waited three quarters of an hour while they finished swinging cargo aboard and setting the hatches to rights. Tugboatmen kill these odd bits of time with cards, and tying up all over the harbor, they know little waterfront stores everywhere which can be reached by froghopping over a series of pilings and climbing a fence or two. Then Carella, as pilot, performed a simple and classic softshoe undocking from Pier F "into the stream," as they say, scrambling down to the *Teresa* again while the Swedes watched. The ship had its running lights on, green on the starboard and red on the port, and the uncountable lights of Manhattan were emerging in all their bravado as the dusk darkened. The water churned between ship and tug; the sea breeze struck us as we slid clear of the ship—the mystically warm-and-cold wind of May.

At sunset we took our flag down, still flying snappily. Our nine-thirty job was to bull back to Greenpoint again and help the *Joan Moran* sail the *Ixia,* an English timber boat. The spray plumed like cream at our bow, and the water was like crinkled tinfoil. The lights of the city were like jubilant news. They were flung out so far that what can one say? They're not man-made; they're the work of some several millions of men. The lights in the office buildings are a blunt blind yellow, blaring into the muffling night, but the lights of Stuyvesant Town and the other big centers of home life are like stippled banks of amber, glowing. I sat on the capstan in the stern, and it was like a whole screwy radar screen. It's so dazzling that one's eyes go dead every minute or so, looking. You can't take it in; you look till your eyes go blank, turn them away to the darker water, and then look again at the sweep of it and the shining water, until again your vision wilts and goes dead.

Over the radio Moran headquarters relayed a suggestion from the *Margot* that we catch up with a self-propelled barge that was running past Williamsburg with virtually no lights on and tell her to hang up a few extra lanterns. But when we did so, the barge captain came out of his cabin and screamed that the regulations had changed and that his dim arrangements were satisfactory. Our captains didn't believe this, so there was some billingsgate of a kind, but since the *Teresa* is not the Coast Guard, we soon went on. Barge captains are the fallen men of the harbor, old drinkers with sorrowful decades at sea behind them, whom you always take care to address as "Captain" every sentence or two.

We roused the mate of the *Ixia* by shining a spotlight along the portholes, then used it to read the draft of the ship for the Sandy Hook pilot so that he would know what he ought to charge. In the spotlight a leaping reindeer on the smokestack came alive, and the smoke, bowel-gray, bulged out of the stack, vaulting and rolling. You don't see so much smoke ashore nowadays. Sometimes I used

87

to go to 13th Street and Avenue D expressly to watch the smoke from the Con Ed stacks jump, flatten, and jump again.

The *Ixia's* hawsers, cast off, hit the water with the smack of rifle reports. Though she is a trim short ship, the slip was narrow, with the heel of another ship just off our stern. The tide was turning, as well; the *Joan's* skipper, acting as pilot, negotiated cautiously. At last, when the ship had been eased out enough, she could start to use her own screw, booting herself briskly out into the stream. We pushed hard on her stern and the *Joan* threw another 4000 horses the opposite way at her bow in order to face her around. The British seamen looked over the rail and let our line down. Their loudspeaker crackled orders to them; and the wind seemed to hit us from the North Sea.

The Moran dispatcher told us to head downriver while he figured out what else to have us do. Finally he said we would have a one-o'clock job—that we should go to Stapleton, Staten Island, and wait for the *Atlantic Saga,* a container ship, which, along with the *Kerry,* we were going to accompany to Port Elizabeth, New Jersey, and dock.

But I shouldn't say "we" any more, because I was dropped off on South Street along the way. Captain Biagi had told me a number of stories that he said I shouldn't print, but now he said that his grandfather had gone on an expedition into the Andes— ". . . one of the first men that ever went into there. And they got lost in the snow. Only two men of the bunch ever came out, you know, including him. And, do you know, he was saved by a St. Bernard dog? That damn dog licking his face. So I owe my life to a St. Bernard! What do you think about that?"

I stood on the bow fender and climbed over the rail at Pier 9, East River, waving good-by and shaking hands, worn out, exuberant, and caught a bus home.

Ten years ago the captains I rode with were Irishmen. In the wheelhouse there was an Irish Mafia, and down in the engine room were the Germans and Danes, usually old merchant seamen who knew the world. The captains lived in Queens Village and looked like Ed Sullivan, and since they'd just started to make lots of money, handling their finances rather scared them, perhaps more than their duties did. I remember one deckhand who was Italian and lived on Prince Street in the Lower East Side and played boccie on his days off. He had just won a bet with his bookie at odds of 140 to 1, but the bookie had only paid off at 50 to 1, claiming that more wasn't possible. It was thought to be part of the fellow's backwardness that he accepted treatment like this from a bookie, or still to be betting on the horses at all, instead of on the market, and playing boccie with the old immigrants. Then the Irishmen would look from him up at the trim heathen Japanese sailors on the many Japanese ships that came in and wonder what in the hell was happening to America that they'd let all these Nips sail into the harbor as freely as that. The captain would clamber down off the ship after docking her, and slanting his eyes with his fingers, imitate the Japanese master gabbling, and do a duckwalk.

There are almost no Negroes on the boats yet. As we went down Manhattan from 23rd Street, every light in the office buildings was on—ranks and ladders of lights like a thousand trombones. All Harlem was there; the cleaning women were working. And the whole city stood on end for me, the light pricks of darkest Brooklyn, the whole grandslam convulsive cacophony. Gradually the black *Ixia* outdistanced us, and a floodlit, ethereal freighter entered the river, as white and as glamorous-looking as some far-ranging knight who can go anywhere and do anything except to stand up or lie down unaided.

ON

NOT BEING

A JEW

M_y girlfriend is trying to decide if I was an Auschwitz guard in order to know how seriously to regard my attentions. She is somewhat old-fashioned, of course, a quality I respect her for, but I don't believe that I was. I believe, in other words, that the Auschwitz guards were Germans, not gentiles. I'm Dutch, as far as that goes. One of my ancestors, a girl of sixteen, was publicly whipped in a market square in New Amsterdam for fornicating with a married man (he was fined). Another, a burgher of the same period, was murdered in a revolt of his slaves. I, for my part, was once fired from a good job for climbing into a mountain lion's cage. I took care of a row of retired MGM lions at the World Jungle Compound in California. MGM adopts as its own one particular lion every year, the year of his clinical prime, which is three to four, and then retires him to the row of cages that I took care of. There was also a mountain lion, a female in heat who called to me at night in my boarding house across the fields with a sound like a pigeon's coo. When I crawled through her door, she went to the back of the cage, turned, and then sprang at me; I simply froze. She darted her football-sized paw into the pale bull's-eye of my face with the claws withdrawn, like a lady's muff. (This was in 1953 and Trader Horn, who was the boss, happened to be passing by and fired me.)

I went to school at various times with Charles Lindbergh's son, Gene Tunney's son, Nelson Rockefeller's son, David Selznick's son, Joseph Kennedy's son, the Aga Khan's son, Henri Matisse's and James Joyce's grandsons; with a Dupont, a Mellon, a Cabot, a Phipps. So what do I have to complain about? Nothing really. I had my lumps to take too, naturally. I spent a great many nights in flophouses in Boston, Pittsburgh, St. Louis, and so on, making up for all this, where an alarm bell rang at nine in the morning and everyone had to be out of the building until five o'clock except for the corps of clean-up trusties. I wrote a term paper at college about one skid row, going to a couple of dozen missions, sitting on the bony benches with the bums, and eating a thin jelly sandwich after the hymns. The Catholics were more generous and easygoing, but I fell for a Grace and Hope nun, a timid hillbilly soprano. At home I'd been required to take lessons in golf at the country club, but I stopped, partly in social revolt and partly because I was on the golf course when a friend of my father's, a liquor company executive, got struck in the groin by a wild ball. He lay on the bench in the locker room as though he'd been hit by a car. The next summer I was traveling with Ringling Bros. and Barnum & Bailey, sleeping in the heap of straw in the giraffe's wagon with a number of battered fellows. When I walked in my sleep they were panic-stricken, thinking the giraffe must have gotten loose and was trampling them. The proprietor's name was Heavy, and because I stuttered he thought that I couldn't understand English, so he would yell, "No sleep, no sleep!" to me, as if to a Chinaman.

My stutter made my teens eventful even on ordinary occasions. Storekeepers were always shoving a paper and pencil at me and then suddenly, deciding I wasn't a mute after all, running around from behind the counter to push me into the street, supposing I must be an epileptic instead. I went to a kind of Yeshiva called Deerfield Academy, which had the oldest headmaster in this hemisphere. He had started the school in 1911 and was an astute power broker, hard on the faculty but a good man, in fact. We called him The Monger; I can't remember why. He gave those of my teachers I especially liked a free hand with me and the years passed quickly enough. One of my friends there is now a traffic manager for Pan Am and I would be at a loss to say what either of us got out of the place, except for straight schooling. We were taught to pick up any scraps of paper we found on the grounds (I don't know who dropped them, but we always seemed to be picking them up), and to look at the sunsets on the western hills.

Sumptuous Harvard was next, where I learned that Pepys is pronounced "peeps" and studied with several extraordinary teachers—MacLeish, Wilder, Ciardi, Kazin, for instance—though I spent an inordinate amount of my hours hanging around Fish Pier and the East Boston docks and the Revere oil refinery. I went to the railroad bridge above the Charlestown State Prison to be enveloped in diesel smoke, and to Copp's Hill, where there was a red-light whorehouse next to the famous burying ground. I used to scuttle past it three or four times in an evening, never able to nerve myself up to go in, until the girls gave up calling to me. As jittery as I was, I needed more rest than my roommate, so I went to bed earlier. I'd masturbate and shortly afterwards he would come in. I'd pretend to be fast asleep so as not to disturb him. He'd masturbate and go to sleep, and then I'd go to sleep.

At Harvard during my freshman year I got to know my first Jews. I tried eagerly to make friends with all that I met, as long as that idea remained plausible, and sometimes their Jewishness was the best thing about them, when, soon after, they turned into bland, buttoned-down types as the sense of being in a minority left them. I had grown up in a suburb of New York where it was next to impossible for a Jew to live. Once, a real estate agent, a red-haired widow, sold one a house and was virtually bankrupted and forced out of business as a result of being ostracized. Another Jewish family somehow contrived to acquire a piece of land, but the neighbors hired a bulldozer to come in and dig a trench around the property to keep their children penned in. It was a strange town. A wealthy elderly lady attempted to leave the community her estate on the noblest-looking of the avenues for a new high school, but this was prep-school territory and in a perfectly open town meeting, New England style, the proposal to accept her gift was voted down. Instead the school was built in a swamp alongside the Merritt Parkway. At the Country Day School we used "jew" as a verb, gigglingly. There were two store owners whose names we recognized as suspect: a Mr. Rosen and Mr. Breslow. Both worked seven days a week (a notion of endless reverberations), and when they retired, the local newspaper confirmed that indeed they'd belonged to the Hebrew faith. Rosen operated a grocery store, so it was our parents who dealt with him, but Mr. Breslow, whose shop was for knicknacks and comic books, we took for our own, some of us stealing, some making phone calls at midnight to him. I myself hung up without saying a word because of my stutter, and then would go to the mirror to look at my nose, which had been described by somebody as Jewish: the thought thrilled me insidiously.

These memories retain the same impress on my mind as being told that it's bad for the eyes to wear rubbers inside the house. They are luminous, permanent. "Never bargain," I was taught at home, and so if I had some object to sell, as when I got rid of my trumpet, I enjoyed bringing it to a pawnshop and bargaining diligently with a Jew. By the age of thirteen, nevertheless, I had picked up two rather remarkable labels: I was a member of the American Society of Ichthyologists and Herpetologists, and I was a socialist. I had known, I think, only one socialist, a humorous man named Gray who lived with his many children in a thirty-room house near us. Actually,

I'd never spoken to him, but I knew that he was a socialist and I stuck to my guns against all argument, although called a commie at school and though every week I spent an absorbed afternoon in the company of *Time* magazine. At Deerfield in 1948 they ran a straw poll. Dewey won something like four hundred thirty-one votes. As for the other candidates—this I'm clear on—Henry Wallace got eight, Truman got three, and Norman Thomas my single vote. An incredulous whoop went up when I gave it. But Deerfield was a sweet-natured 1910 place by comparison with my hometown, where I fought many tearful, furious fights. They might be on unionization or the minimum wage, but anti-Semitism was generally detectable in the discussion. Though Negroes were only a laughing matter, Jews were not, and quite correctly so, because in a few years Leonard Bernstein was to be the New York Philharmonic's conductor, publicly kissing the President's wife (this was the worst), and Arthur Goldberg would have caught Kennedy's ear instead of the silly Bernie Baruch. Even the town itself, as a bastion, fell when the developers built too many houses for the sales to be closely controlled. Today the population has tripled from the hometown I knew, and if there still aren't many such outright and shameless stark names as Cohen or Gould in the telephone book, a number of ambiguous forerunners—Wolfs, Millers and Whites—have appeared.

Meanwhile, I was out in the West fighting forest fires in a hotshot crew, or mopping the basement of Madison Square Garden when the circus was there. Lindbergh's son, I used to hear, was paddling a kayak on Long Island

Sound, camping out winter and summer. Another boy I went to school with went up to Fairbanks, Alaska, and became a world authority on grizzly bears. My college roommate, having read Thoreau, was solving our masturbatory difficulties by sleeping rolled up in a khaki blanket on the floor of the sitting room. On the other hand, my best friend at Deerfield had made the unfortunate mistake of reading a lot of late Tolstoy, had quit school to live on the Lower East Side, and was giving the shirts off his back to every addict who asked for one, until he wound up in a mental hospital.

I was a bit Tolstoyan too. I lived in that neighborhood later on, watching the games of stoop-ball, the kids swimming off the piers downtown, the beatniks who lived overswept by stray cats with a sign in the window: "Have you ever owned a painting?—20¢." On the street I would lean down and feel the pulse of a bum who was lying unconscious to make sure his problem was liquor.

The lives led by the very poor are not very much more harassed than the lives which middle-class people lead. It's the crampedness, the developing paranoia, that make poor people so wretched—never getting away for a trip, never enjoying any real relaxation, new scenes, new distractions. Wagner and Lehman campaigned through the Lower East Side with apologetic, uneasy expressions, looking like older men than they did uptown, like men who wished to retire and let somebody else try to fix these problems. Once when I'd sprained my ankle I realized how dangerous the neighborhood could be, because I couldn't run—couldn't even walk briskly through the most depressing streets like Third Street, which was spattered with puke and broken glass, where the Emergency Home for men was located. But it was also where hot-dog push-carts loaded up, and you would see the full-bearded patriarchs who did the pushing extinguishing their char-coal at the end of the day to get some use out of the coals tomorrow. You'd see a police car cruise by and a boy on a tricycle peddling as fast as he could alongside with his arm raised in greeting. I lived next to an artisan locksmith who taxied all over the city to jobs or else worked in front of our building on a succession of cars, having the driver lock him in the trunk, where he could pick his way free. Sometimes he seemed superbly human, sometimes scarcely human at all because he worked so hard. He had a slouchy Z posture, gnarled blocky fingers, the earnest face of a clever groundhog, and a fat chest he folded his arms on when he was talking. His main tool was just a tap-hammer, and he could have walked into any bank and begun to work on the locks without being asked to show his credentials; he looked like an incontrovertible lock-smith, an honest master.

We alumni of the Lower East Side pour out stories when we get together as if we were at a college reunion —especially those of us who are in a position to go to college reunions. Plenty of girls from my sort of back-ground were there, girls metamorphosed into wan social workers; and some went overboard and married a sandal-maker of thirty-eight or a man obsessed with clocks and axes. I was too much of a waffler to turn into a drastic Tolstoyan, and besides I'd been out in the fresh air for years, learning the truck drivers' language of headlight flicks and benedictions conveyed with a roll of the hand.

The first girl I kissed was an innkeeper's daughter in Pittsfield, Mass. (I wrote her a letter of self-abasement afterwards which her mother steamed open.) The second girl lived next door to me in a hotel in Cleveland. Three days before, she had escaped from a coal-mining town in the Appalachians where they spit on the floor of the fire hall, watching the weekly movie; and she crossed the clattering streets holding my hand as if we were wading into big breakers. We went to the Palace Theater, with its chandeliers, mirrors and thick pile rugs, as if we'd inherited a mighty sum.

It wasn't until my mid-twenties that I could volunteer where I was from: until then, I said "near Stamford" or "from Connecticut." But all this adventuring, the clumsy penance of living in Negro hotels on upper Broadway, makes me a confident WASP nowadays without any apologies for what I am. As a matter of fact, I'm not a WASP—my name is Americanized Dutch—but I'm lumped with the Anglo-Saxons as carelessly as we in that bedroom suburb would have classified an Armenian with the rest of the Jews. WASP is a pejorative word, a sociological equivalent of dago or kike. W.P., for white Protestant, certainly can have a legitimate meaning, but the A.S. in the middle has been added gratuitously for kicks. Everyone took to the word at first, but lately, oddly enough, the people who use it the most are themselves WASPs, often boot-me's who relish the sensation of turn-about, or else those like myself who say it ironically, as a black man will say he's a nigger. Usually Jews, sensing its disparaging connotations and remembering kike, avoid the word as non-U, though they may be content that it exists.

Anyway, as a WASP, I found that my tearful battles when I was thirteen on behalf of social justice, or whatever it might be considered to be, were wholly beside the point, to put it mildly. I saved no householder his house, and history was marching swiftly along. No doubt some of my classmates who remained placidly anti-Semitic until they were of voting age are freer of the memory of those early catechisms than I. Recently my mother asked me why so many of the writers interviewed on TV appear to be Jews; I said because probably most writers are Jews. It was a new world for me, New York in the late 1950s. To be a Jew must have been like being a Yorkshireman if you were a young English writer— the vigor was said to be yours; the eyes were on you. I found I was kind of an Ibo, an ornament, in some circles, though welcome enough. My fair skin and glossy hair were commented on by every girlfriend. That scene from Saul Bellow's *The Victim* must have been enacted two dozen times—someone would reach out and touch my hair in the midst of an unrelated conversation. Of course I was no victim; I was doing quite well for myself. The girls thought sex might be better with me and I thought sex might be better with them. They would try to decide what to cook for me that I would feel at home with, and end up doing Indian pudding; afterwards they would marvel, practically catch their breath, at the literal cross the hair forms on my chest. It was fun and tender and serious too, no longer mere experimentation. I did grow a bit bored at being taught *chutzpah* and *mensch* and *shlepping* so regularly; no one seemed to realize that everybody was teaching these words to people like me. Usually the teacher herself had only just learned them, but they were ethnically hers, and the idea was that some of their extraordinary vigor might be imparted to me if I ingested them. A person who knew how to say *chutzpah* could develop *chutzpah* even if he weren't Jewish.

I could make a good many obvious jokes about all of this, but later when I spent a year in British Columbia, where the whites were either Scottish or Irish, I would have embraced anybody who'd walked up to me whispering in Yiddish. And in New York I was learning, meanwhile, about the slaughter of six million Jews. During the war we gentiles had heard in detail about the Japanese concentration camps but very little about the German camps, and although some time along in my teens I had figured out for myself the astounding information that Christ was a Jew, this other news was not news you could figure out. There were large and terrific reasons for the surge of Jewish identity or pride, and maybe those Jews who had never wondered where they wanted their roots to be needed more patience than I during the process of self-discovery. People who had changed their names wished that they hadn't done so. Jews my age simply were saying the word "Jew" a great deal, as if they had never said it before, trying the sound of it in their mouths. The most Protestantized Ivy League fellows began to teach me *chutzpah,* and everybody in New York who wasn't a Jew was marrying one, just as everybody who was a Jew was marrying a gentile.

One way or another it was as intriguing to be a Jew as it was precarious. I was walking on Broadway on the afternoon Jack Ruby shot Lee Harvey Oswald. You could breathe the hushed, gingerly triumph. One old man of the many who'd hastily rushed out to the street came up to me. "Did you hear Oswald got shot?" I said yes. "Yeah, a Jew shot him!" he said gleefully. *Now they'll have to respect us!* Before he began to imagine horrible pogroms, Ruby's logic is reported to have been the same. A liberal people who have been belittled become confused, the intellectuals too, as when Israel achieved her lightning conquest in 1967 and suddenly sat astraddle so much territory. She'd had to win but now she was *bigger.* Being bigger, and the prowess of victory, supplanted having to win, like a shrill bugling.

During the fifties, at the same time as my work was beginning to be published, there was a historic coming of age of American Jewish writing. Malamud after *The Natural,* Bellow after *Dangling Man,* Kazin after *On Native Grounds* went out and wrote much more than brilliantly; they wrote differently, establishing a new tradition, indeed a new establishment. To a young writer three establishments were apparent. The Southerners, leaning heavily on the greatness of Faulkner and on their own social graces, didn't especially interest me, except for Faulkner himself. *The New Yorker* paid its contributors lavish honorariums but seemed a dying institution. It had the phenomenal John Updike, a brilliant throwback prodigiously equipped, and the admirable workhorse John Cheever, and the frail, phosphorescent J. D. Salinger, who wrote as if he were chipping mica. I had grown up reading Melville, Whitman, Dreiser and Faulkner, and the next in line for me was Saul Bellow. Malamud, slightly less gifted, pulled even with him in certain short masterpieces because of the clarity and incandescence of his themes, but when Bellow had a theme going for him, as in *Henderson the Rain King* and in *Seize the Day,* I read him most avidly. We were finally introduced by the affectionate poet John Berryman, and took to each other, he becoming a friend by correspondence and a faithful reader, so that as far as I could see there was no question of this establishment being exclusive (as Gore Vidal has complained). Other than Bellow, the novelists I encountered who went out of their way to make kindly gestures to me were people like Philip Roth and Harvey Swados.

The burst of concentrated enthusiasm for writers consciously Jewish couldn't help having an effect, however. I think that Cheever received less attention than he deserved for several years while he was at the height of his powers, and maybe the recognition due other writers was also delayed. For youngsters like Updike or John Barth it didn't matter as much. The push of their talent was only beginning, and a lean fox catches more rabbits. In my own case, my first novel came out about the same month as Sam Astrakhan's *An End to Dying,* which was about immigrant family life, shifting from the Ukraine

103

to the garment center. Both were pretty fair books, he was a friend of many of my friends, and I remember being startled and disconcerted by how completely they gave their immediate attention to him. Being reviewed well, though, I was happy, and, in any event, the only bad effect of non-recognition to a writer at that stage of the game is when he can't publish what he has written while it is still important to him, a trouble that generally I didn't have. I dealt with a couple of magazine editors who expressed surprise when I mentioned Bellow's liking my stuff ("You? He *does?*") and who turned their moo-cow eyes on me intently when I allowed as how I felt an affinity for him. "But he's so *unhappy*," one said, meaning in his role of suffering Jew.

In the meantime Philip Roth was having problems quite the reverse. After the howl of hosanna for *Goodbye Columbus,* which is a splendid book, he was able to publish practically anything and would sometimes wonder whether he should. He'd done the first widely read satire of a genre of Jewish-American life, and so the false expectation was raised that each of his succeeding books must be a first. It seems to me that along with Barth and Updike he's the best writer now in his thirties we have; I think he knows the most about people. But he was penalized in the responses to *Letting Go* and *When She Was Good* for that initial hosanna. Some critics say that Henry Roth should have received an instant hosanna too, in the 1930s, for *Call It Sleep,* and regard his career as pitifully blighted. I agree that his book deserved cymbals and clangor, but writing is a spartan, bloody profession and I think if he'd had further books in him they would have come out—like Nelson Algren's, which were just as neglected, although his first two books are nearly as gracefully written as his middle two; like Nathanael West's; like Faulkner's, who in 1944 is said to have been listed only twice in the central card catalogue of the New York libraries.

One thing *did* matter to somebody like me, classified as a WASP writer. This was being told in print and occasionally in person that I and my heritage lacked vitality, that except perhaps for a residual arrogance the vitality had long ago been squeezed dry—if in fact it had ever existed in thin blood like mine. I was a museum piece, like some State of Mainer, because I could field no ancestor who had hawked copper pots in a Polish *shtetl*. Obviously talk like that can grow fur on a stone! I looked up old photographs of my great-grandfathers in Kansas, their faces unsteady and mad as John Brown's, and recognized an equivalent rashness in me. I had a riverboat captain on the Ohio for a relative; another, a naval cook in the Boxer Rebellion, sprang ashore from his ship and was the first man shot dead.

But the decade is past when even the zealous take note of which writer is Jewish and which is not. Instead, the question has shifted around to who is a writer at all. We go to the movies now, or read the lyrics on the back of the Beatles' record albums. It's certainly quicker than reading a book; and we all go to poetry readings because we can catch a taste of the young fellow's personality without actually needing to bite a chunk out of his work.

Allen Ginsberg is the new Carl Sandburg. Blessings on both: Sandburg was quite a stage man himself. But the concept of taking a poet's vocal abilities so seriously we've borrowed from the Russians, forgetting that they hold their readings as a dismal if defiant substitute for a free press. Hardly two years ago novelists who were having trouble with their work, the talented but chronic under-performers, were going into book-length journalism, which was supposed to be the form of the future. Now it's the Easy Arts that are in—easy for viewer, easy for artist. Who wants to read books any more—unless it's zany pornography? *The Graduate* replaces *Bonnie and Clyde* replaces *La Guerre Est Finie* as Book-of-the-Month. We writers are told that the novel is moribund, that we're working in a dead language; time is short, people are listening to glugging guitarists and aren't going to spend it curled up with a book. I doubt that we're going to be told this for long, but if I am wrong, if we do find that our language at last is certified dead, then I think that we will draw strength from our privacy, as Isaac Bashevis Singer has, and precisely because of that privacy, some of us will irradiate and transcend translation.

THE
DRAFT CARD
GESTURE

A month has gone by since I sent my draft card to President Johnson, "symbolically torn in half," as I put it to him. I had written him a more fully reasoned letter ten months before that, and I wanted to transfer myself from one category of dissenters to another one, since the war had gone on. I have no spare card to look at to see what penalties I am liable for. In theory they are fearsome enough, but probably I won't be liable for any, being already thirty-five and a veteran besides. Nobody has visited me. If I had really thought the FBI would become energetically concerned I might not have made the gesture. The last year or so of my two Army years was nearly as stultified in routine as prison must be and I wouldn't want to repeat the experience. I lead a more codified life now, whereas when I was a boy everything was grist to me.

Like many people, I had been looking for a gesture, some concise, limited act which suited me in some way and whose consequences would not be unboundedly grave. One laconic dove I am acquainted with calls this sort of thing therapy, like the professors who shout at recruiters for Dow. Admittedly it is; many of us are losing our cool. The Frenchman who watched the drawn-out, appalling Algerian War at least had a flux of developments to contend with and a change of personae, not Secretary Rusk for seven years. Nevertheless, although I would do it again for lack of a better idea, I'm not very comfortable with my gesture. It's a glove thrown down that won't be picked up, and it seems falsely, deliberately youthful. I might instead have signed the statement which is available for people who are withholding their income taxes, but I didn't do that because the nit-picking tangle of red tape that would result seemed more distressing to contemplate than even a possible FBI visit. I have no accountant to help me and I decided the tax protest wasn't my style.

Of course I've marched several times, accepting the anomalies of those occasions—the *Workers* distributed, the teenagers begging for trouble, the simplistic slogans ("Hell, no, we won't go!"). My first march was the great March on Washington in 1963 which crested so much civil-rights accomplishment. I rode down to that in an ancient school bus full of white youngsters who sang *Old Black Joe*. And yet they were not merely gauche. They converted the driver, who had started the day like a typical union man driving a busload of kooks, and they sang *We Shall Overcome* so fervently that the maids in the motels stopped working as we went by. When we pulled

into the parking lot at the Washington Monument, reporters surrounded us. "Free–dom," chanted our group,
which sounded like "We've come," which would have
been equally good. The Mississippi contingent marched
the length of the mall more than once because they felt
they had earned it and because it was a thrill. The police
captains beamed as at a fish fry for kids, the city people
sneezed with hay fever, the Monument stood gleaming
and tall, and happy-looking clergymen stood about everywhere, more happy clergy than had ever gathered before
anywhere. The wit of Wilkins, the shivering exhortations
of King were enhanced fantastically by the fact that two
hundred thousand people had collected here for the sake
of an urgent dream that in some of its practical, easier
aspects was on the brink of being achieved. We had a
flexible President, we had a national consensus that the
time for this change had come due. It was a day of lavish,
exhilarating courtesy—of the Golden Rule. Our cheeks
felt pouchy with backed-up tears; our throats throbbed the
whole afternoon. The crowd carried the day—the speakers
took the crowd's cue. Afterwards I flew home. In the airport washroom there was a wretched moment when I
tried to persuade a Negro traveler to break a dollar bill
for me, assuming that he was the bootblack because he
was black. I had no change because I had tipped the cab
driver well, and I'd tipped him well because he had
undercharged me. He'd undercharged me because, on
impulse, I had sat in the front seat with him; and so the
day ended appropriately complicatedly. But, just as these
exercises would seem like playing games in the context

of Black Power, the very idea of trekking to Washington in that hopeful and peaceful mood, believing that as Americans we could evoke a government response, was part of the year 1963.

In October that fall there was a March on City Hall which I joined when it passed my street. It was a ragtag, provocative bunch of angry young militants and painfully fired-up older Negroes, in some cases drunk. "Wagner must go!" was the yell. We avoided looking at one another as we walked, and the police mocked us. None of the featured speakers showed up. The reporters for the *Daily News* grinned. Then, the summer of 1964 was the first summer of riots, the worst in New York since the Second World War. An eerie, gingerly city noticed the line-up of blacks to whites on each subway car. The radio broadcast a Roman roar from 125th Street, and even downtown I saw considerable violence and was almost arrested a couple of times for sticking my nose in, when the Negroes would dodge out from under the policemen's clubs and get away. I saw police beaten up too: much sad courage.

Civil rights splintered confusingly as a cause, and the tiny, vestigial ear for suffering that might be remedied which many of us possess became more attuned to the Vietnam war. The bulky march in April 1967 to the UN was a pleasant stroll, but the memorable exuberance of the '63 march was gone. We knew we were shouting to a deaf ear, and few of us had seen Vietnam, nobody was Vietnamese, so that even the imagery in our minds was thwarted and inaccurate. At the end of the year, the one draft demonstration at Whitehall which I sampled was still harder for me to unite myself with. *"If the horses are charging you, move in a zigzag pattern. If the horses are standing still, put your hands on their noses and they will not charge you."* (At the Washington March in 1963 we'd been instructed to eat our mayonnaise sandwiches before noon so that they wouldn't spoil and make us ill.) It was a predawn army with hectoring marshals, a hurry-up-wait atmosphere, and a certain hysteric camaraderie. Plain-clothes detectives with pinprick green buttons in their lapels were everywhere. Dawn arrived, sunrise came. Police and students acted equally belligerently. The police herded us continually, as if enjoying it, rapping their clubs on the wooden barriers. The setting was an attractive, elderly area faced in old stone, and the massed shouts echoed up out of unison like the shouts of the Civil War draft riots there. By eight in the morning the office workers began pouring through, perturbed and scolding, because this wasn't a matter of challenging racial prejudices which they already quite recognized were outdated and contradictory—this was dissent; this was calling an American war an unjust war, a phenomenon unknown to the national experience for a hundred years. I was dressed conventionally but wearing a flower, and on the subway going home I met hundreds of questioning stares.

I wrote my covering letter to the President, saying that one could not forever protest a ferocious war by what are called peaceful means, and attaching the two scraps of the draft card with a paper clip, dropped the letter into the mail chute of my building, listening to its descent. I had been carrying the card since 1950, when Edith

111

Moriarty of Norwalk, Connecticut, signed it for me. To an extent, I had shared the bewilderment of many of the policemen at Whitehall and the starers on the subway because, like them, I was a veteran. I knew that the experience of military service was usually a useful one and, looking around, I could see whom it might have been particularly useful to. Although I live differently now than I did in 1955 when I was waiting to be drafted, even taking me as I was then, there would have been some dissimilarities between my attitude and that of a lot of the kids on the March. I was a direct patriot, a peppy, idealistic fellow living off Union Square. I had hitchhiked all over America, dragging my suitcase through forty-three states. I'd seen the Snake and the Rio Grande, and San Diego and Aberdeen, Wash.; in fact I'd turned down a trip to Europe in order to go out and see more. And so in the evenings I often went to the Square to hear the accents of the soapbox speakers, scanning the wheat-belt and Kentucky faces. It seemed that the entire country was represented there, old men of every occupation, scallop boatmen and soybean farmers. The Communists spoke under an equestrian statue—"under the horse's ass," as they said. Early birds saved the platform for them and they scheduled themselves: first a small dedicated Jewish bookkeeper who spoke seriously from notes; after him, a rangy Dos Passos Communist with Idaho still in his voice and the vocal cords of a labor organizer; and lastly a Khrushchev Communist, an emotive, fair-minded Russian, a family man with an earthy, demonstrative face who rode up from Catherine Street on his bicycle with a white terrier running alongside. They were assigned by the party—even the early birds—to the task, they told us. The other speakers hadn't the training or the podium, but they did their best: a prototype black nationalist, a hollering atheist, a thin Catholic proselytizer who was a retired businessman living on West 72nd Street—he was the odd man out and he tore his voice shouting at all of them. They brought up the Inquisition so many times that at last he started defending it. There were also a couple of opera singers, a vaudeville comedian, and a pacifist who knelt on the pavement after every pugnacious remark that he made. One man, a turkey-necked, pasty-cheeked fellow of fifty, couldn't speak at all; apparently his throat had been operated on. His opponents would give him the floor anyway. Bending down next to his mouth to catch his whisper, they repeated it to the crowd and then answered it.

I loved Dos Passos and Steinbeck, and though my blood beat at the stories of injustice the crowd was told, mainly I came to the square because of the faces I saw, constituting a map of the continent, from the tunafish cannery where I'd worked one July to the Platte River that I'd hitchhiked along. As a matter of fact, I didn't have to be drafted. I chose to be drafted for a number of reasons, one of which was this heated enthusiasm of mine for America as a whole—I loved the pink deserts; I could distinguish a Milwaukee accent from a Cincinnati drawl. But since I was subject to asthma during the summer and stuttered, both ailments which offered me a legitimate out, for more than a year I'd been debating whether to

113

become 4-F or 1-A. When I leaned toward the first choice, however, my asthma reared up and almost asphyxiated me and I stuttered so badly I became mute. I did want to go into the Army for the loving, elated reasons that Steinbeck might have felt, but quite beyond them I realized I *had* to go in. Whether from a sense of guilt or from doubt of my competence as a man otherwise, if I didn't I would be troubled for years afterwards.

The day of the physical came at last. The doctor already had records that would have let me out, but talking as smoothly as Simon Peter, I asked him please to ignore them; I told him I was all right. In basic training I gained twenty pounds and completely stopped stuttering for a while. The jammed early months were a sort of bazaar of cornpone youngsters, sturdy black sergeants, close-order instruction and capsuled war games. At Fort Sam Houston I slept underneath an undertaker. I had porky best friends and skinny best friends, who were perfume chemists and lathe operators. Then I was sent to Pennsylvania, where I stayed twenty months, engrossed in writing a novel whenever I could. The supercharged excitement petered out; I became my accustomed neurotic self.

As long as I actually remained in the Army I wasn't too smug or moralistic about serving because I wasn't entirely glad about it. But when the period was over I grew raucous and difficult for those of my friends who had chosen to huddle in graduate school or had painted their toenails red for the draft exam. I thought they'd denied themselves one of the core experiences. I still think they did, and I'm sorry that so many boys nowadays find it necessary to avoid that first salubrious shock of a training camp—the self-discoveries, the fortuitous friendships, the vaccinal dip in the stewpan of war. But it seems necessary that they do so. This war is too atrociously twisted in its rationale to have been declared. It has become as meaningful now to tear one's draft card in half as it once was to insist upon being drafted. Strong patriots are going to jail, and if I remain anonymous as a number in a file at the Justice Department, at least I have dramatized my dissent by removing myself from a prosaic list to a red-letter list.

BOOKS, MOVIES,
THE NEWS

I am commencing an undertaking, hitherto without precedent, and which will never find an imitator. I desire to set before my fellows the likeness of a man in all the truth of nature, and that man myself.
Myself alone! I know the feelings of my heart, and I know men. I am not made like any of those I have seen; I venture to believe that I am not like any of those in existence.

So says Rousseau, beginning his *Confessions*. Whitman began *Song of Myself* as boldly, and any number of the classic writers, however opposite their philosophies, might have set off in much the same spirit, for instance the modest Defoe when he wrote *Moll Flanders* or *Robinson Crusoe:* "I am commencing an undertaking without precedent." All literature was a great gold field and, only limited by their energies, these individuals of talent had all the free play they could ask for. Rousseau, besides believing he was writing the first catch-as-catch-can *Confessions* and that nobody else would ever try such an enterprise again, actually thought that he was a man unlike any other! We who write nowadays can only goggle. We have three and a half billion people on earth just at present, and even if the figure were a fraction of that, the sciences of the psyche have long since shown us how we are peas in a pod, so that high art seeks mainly to capture the terms of

116

our common humility. This wouldn't matter so much to a writer if he were surer that at least in his own work he was digging new ground. What hasn't been done and said by now?—even in regard to technique alone, is the newest work new? Babe Ruth and Hemingway flourished in an era of single performers and ample time, but now more people want to write novels than are willing to read them; there's a glut in the stores, a glut in the mind. Some novelists continue in the old disciplines of Forster and Joyce, while others do capsule, doomsday burlesques of everything that has gone before, considering that all the world's books have already been written. Perhaps John Barth's *The Sotweed Factor* is the best of these, and Steven Schneck's *The Nightclerk* applies a somewhat equivalent *force de frappe* to pornography.

Diaries are another method of writing that is in vogue, as old as the hills and yet as contemporary as Sirhan Sirhan, whose scrabbled jottings had been published before by Evan S. Connell and John Fowles. Diaries are a means of writing in the present tense, which is what writers are tempted to do. The news leaps right alongside us, baying, today, and is so innovative that literary invention is put to the test just to keep stride. Charles Manson, Commander Bucher, Abe Fortas, Rap Brown: daily installments are serialized, bite-sized, as if by an expert teaser, and as the news-gathering apparatus improves, more and more people are born, too, producing more newsworthy vagaries. Norman Mailer makes news, partakes in its very inception, in order to write that close to events, and though he doesn't say that the world's novels have already been written, his methods are testimony to that effect. This is rather a serious business, because both Mailer and Barth probably have more raw talent than any other writers alive.

Ortega y Gasset's *Notes on the Novel* has a subchapter, "Decline and Perfection," suggesting that the last years of an art may be its most pure. "In the great hour of the decline of the genre . . . the opportunity of achieving the perfect work is excellent . . . when accumulated experience has utterly refined the artistic sensitivity." Certainly most novelists would prefer this view, if simply to keep their hopes up. But a firmer strongpoint for the writer to put his back to is the fact that prose has no partitions now. Fiction is semi-fiction, and the whole mix of stemwinding collage-reportage, stripped-down fable, elegiac celebration and stern, unindulgent character study, the passion and clarity of poetic technique and the muddy, yanking tenacity of the autobiographical novelist can clinch together in the same piece of work. No forms exist any more, except that to work as a single observer, using the resources of only one mind, and to work with words—this is being a writer.

Reading a book amounts to being talked to alone by somebody else for a long time; but we've become impersonal lately, we chat in groups, we don't usually spend time in this way. Movies move, streaming over the screen in soothing darkness for ninety minutes, like a product of many hands, whereas books, which have the logistics of a private art, must be pulled out of the page by the reader, who to some extent recapitulates the labor of the author himself. And though it used to be that writers who needed money would go to Hollywood and work as a cool hand on a sad script, now they take the procedure more seriously, regarding the screen treatment of even their own books as a continuation of the artistic process. All those cameras—maybe it is. Yet so far, until the concomitants of financing can be got under control, filmmaking is like applied research, because the men who make quality movies still search through the bookstores as through a seedbed. Any novelist who lives accessibly in the city has talked with the free-lance operatives who hunt about town for a cheap option on a good book—has talked to them with a combination of sympathy and bemusement, since they're often hungrier than he. They're on the prowl for ideas, believing that he is still the repository of ideas that embody the skid of the times, and storytelling ideas—if he hasn't an inside track, at least he works like an honest mule.

There aren't any Maxwell Perkins types to help him along. Editors don't stay long enough at a given publishing house to nurture a writer (the writers themselves don't stay), and if *The New Yorker*'s identifiable editorial regime has hand-raised a few fine fellows in recent years, the effect on them may have been limiting rather than bracing. Anyway, *New Yorker* writers have tended to be country boys since the beginning. If they don't come from Columbus, Ohio (and it's remarkable how many do), they are from financially pinched but genteel circumstances which generated a need for elegance, moral support and a dependable income even while they were fledglings. Novelists lead swampier lives. Between books they look in the telephone book to see if their name is in print anywhere, and they sign on for a stint of three or four years with a publishing house before moving painfully on to another one. They're lame-legged creatures with swollen lungs, forced as a rule to announce their own achievements (if any) in personal advertisements of some kind or other because most of the critics are writing about the movies. Kurosawa's ragtag, misdoubting seven samurai furnish an image of the novelist's position—his craft corrupted by the swarm of practitioners, himself disgruntled, outdated and poor. His traditional role has been to tell us how we live, a task which already by the last century had grown too topheavy for the essayist or playwright. But with the best will in the world he can't really hope to do this now; a computer bank like the A.P.–U.P.I. is needed. Besides the daily tattoo of such lurid figures as Spiro Agnew, we have earth slides in Turkey and Santa Ana, heart transplants around the world, aquanauts in two oceans, astronauts by the dozen, riots in China, Czechoslovakia and Ireland; we have Picasso; we have the birds and the oil slicks; we have the war between the old and young. Our gossip is not drawn so much from the missteps of our neighbors as from this enormous Oriental rug of a novel, stitched together by TV and Telex—the misery of Biafra, the fall of the last of the Kennedys. As wild reality it calls upon the madcap paroxysms of all the millions in every time zone, smothering the established pleasures of fiction. Novels are no longer cliff-hangers or "rich" by comparison, and no one who pretends to be alive, nobody who enjoys reading the broad-beamed books of the nineteenth century, can help poring over the newspaper. A writer trying to match its seethe and improvisation is like John Henry: gallant but doomed. Writing in the instant tense, he may contrive to paraphrase or mimic it for the moment, but what is his one effort of the imagination when set against the steam drill of those millions—any one of whom, by an inspired spasm, will have his name chattered around the world?

Of course a book can be highlighted, can be stark, and can be art—complete in a way that just the pizzicato facts can never be. It is an excellent development for prose as well as for the novel that demarcations between the forms have blurred, because the emphasis is on the single mind, the *private* mind, and this will be the strength of writing and the other private arts when the real stress-fatigue sets in at the brutality of population growth—we're going to be so awfully sick of seeing what is being seen by ninety million other people the same week.

At its best, reading is like the swimming described in Greek epics. Odysseus swam for two days and nights; Poseidon sent a cold current against him; Athena warmed him with the sun; Poseidon heaved up giant waves to bash him under; but Athena countered with an easterly wind and the sea grew calm. If novels don't provide the kind of spread a wide screen does, they give the roomy living space which privacy requires. Since this space has to be incompressible, in the struggle to keep it so the arts of single sensibility are going to reacquire a power.

For even the defeats of a good writer are plaintive—Saul Bellow overcome occasionally by the same incoherence he celebrates, or Nabokov appearing as a Hitchcock pixie when he is out of phase. And movements in literature are always personal. During the past forty years the Scott Fitzgerald themes of making it, and the nature of talent itself, have vied in many variants with the Dos Passos example of social concern. There are a lot of young Dos Passoses around again, though most of them have scarcely started writing yet, but members of the Fitzgerald party are aging and out, and so it rather looks as if the Dos Passos group will vie with Barth and Günter Grass, and that all parties will confront especially the news, catapulting raw meat hunks like a pitching machine.

We have the public arts, exemplified by the movies, the private arts, and the explosions of news. To ignore the news would be to lose interest in life itself, but the arts depict man as he is alone. Not only is he still alone, but for the first time ever he is beginning an era when he will *wish* to be alone.

THE THRESHOLD
AND THE
JOLT OF PAIN

Like most boys in their teens, I wondered once in a while how I would take torture. Badly, I thought. Later I thought not so badly, as I saw myself under the pressures of danger or emergency, once when a lion cub grabbed my hand in its mouth and I wrestled its lips for half a minute with my free hand. Another summer when I fought forest fires in a crew of Indians in the West, we stood up under intense heat and thirst, watching the flames crackle toward us irresistibly while we waited to see whether the fire lines that we had cut were going to hold. I've climbed over the lip of a high waterfall; I've scratched inside a hippopotamus's capacious jaws; I faced a pistol one day in Wyoming with some degree of fortitude. However, I knew that all this élan would vanish if my sex organs were approached. The initiation to join the Boy Scouts in our town was to have one's balls squeezed, so I never joined. Even to have my knuckle joints ground together in a handshake contest reduces me to quick surrender—something about bone on bone. I steered clear of the BB-gun fights in my neighborhood, and I could be caught in a chase and tied up easily by someone slower who yelled as if he were gaining ground, so I made friends with most of the toughies as a defensive measure.

As a boy I was much given to keeping pets and showering care on them, but I had a sadistic streak as well. In boarding school my roommate got asthma attacks when he was jumped on, and I always backed away laughing when his tormentors poured into the room. There was another nice boy whom I seldom picked on myself, and with sincere horror I watched a game grip the Florentine fancy of our corridor. Divided in teams, we would push him back and forth as a human football from goal to goal. The crush at the center, where he was placed, was tremendous, and though no one remembered, I'd invented the game.

My first love affair was with a Philadelphian, a girl of twenty-seven. That is, she was the first girl I slept with. She was a love in the sense that she loved me; I was close and grateful to her but didn't love her—I'd loved one girl earlier whom I hadn't slept with. She lived in one of those winsome houses that they have down there, with a tiled backyard and three floors, one room to each floor. We wandered along the waterfront and spent Saturdays at the street market, which is the largest and visually the richest street market in the United States. I was not an ogre to her, but I did by stages develop the habit of beating her briefly with my belt or hairbrush before we made love, a practice which I have foregone ever since. It may be indicative of the preoccupations of the 1950s that I worried less about this than about any tendencies I may have had toward being homosexual; but the experience gives me a contempt for pornography of that arch gruesome genre, quite in vogue nowadays as psychological "exploration," where whipping occurs but the flesh recovers its sheen overnight and the whippee doesn't perhaps hang her(him)self, propelling the whipper into the nervous breakdown which he is heading for.

Seeing eventual disaster ahead, I didn't go deeply into this vein of sensation, just as I was shrewd enough as a boy not to be picked on often or to suffer more than a few accidents. Once I ran my hand through an apple crusher, and once I imitated a child's stutter at summer camp, thereby—or so I imagined (remembering what was supposed to happen to you if you crossed your eyes)— picking up the malady at the age of six. Almost my only pangs, then, were this stutter, which still remains in my mouth. It may strike other people as more than a spasm, but to me it's a spasm of pain of a kind which I haven't time for, or time to regard as anything else. It's like someone who has a lesion or twist in his small intestine, which hurts him abruptly and of which he is hardly aware otherwise. The well-grooved wince I make in shaking the words out seems to keep my face pliant and reasonably young.

Somerset Maugham described his bitter discovery when he was a boy that prayer was no help: he woke up next morning still clamped to his adamant stutter. I was more of a pantheist; I kept trusting to the efficacy of sleep

itself, or to the lilting lift that caused birds to fly. Also I
went to a bunch of speech therapists. At the Ethical Culture School in New York, for example, a woman taught
me to stick my right hand in my pocket and, with that
hidden hand, to write down over and over the first letter
of the word I was stuttering on. This was intended to dis-
tract me from stuttering, and it did for a week or
two. The trouble was that watching me play pocket pool
that way was more unsettling to other people than the
ailment it was meant to cure. At a camp in northern
Michigan I was trained by a team from the university to
speak so slowly that in effect I wasn't speaking at all; I
talked with the gradualism of a flower growing—so
absurdly tardy a process that my mind unhinged itself
from what was going on. In Cambridge, Massachusetts, a
young fellow from the University of Iowa—and oh, how
he stuttered—took the most direct approach. He got me
to deliberately imitate myself, which was hard on me since
I was already terribly tired of stuttering, and to stare, as
well, at the people whom I was talking to in order to find
out what their reactions were. I found out, for one thing,
that some of my friends and about a fifth of the strangers
I met smiled when the difficulty occurred, though they
generally turned their heads to the side or wiped their
mouths with one hand to hide the smile. Thereafter, life
seemed simpler if I avoided looking at anybody, whoever
he was, when I was stuttering badly, and I wasn't so
edgily on the alert to see if I'd spit inadvertently.

Not that I lacked understanding for the smilers, though,
because for many years I too had had the strange im-

pulse, hardly controllable, to smile if somebody bumped his head on a low door lintel or received sad news. The phenomenologists say this is a form of defense. It goes with childhood especially, and I stopped indulging in it one night in Boston when I was in a police patrol wagon. A friend and I had been out for a walk, he was hit by a car, and as he woke from unconsciousness during the ride to the hospital and asked what had happened, I found myself grinning down at him while I answered. A few weeks later I was walking past an apartment building just as a rescue squad carried out a would-be suicide. He was alive, on a stretcher. When our eyes touched he smiled impenetrably, but I didn't smile back.

As a stutterer, I learned not to write notes. You put yourself at someone's mercy more when you write him a note than if you just stand there like a rhinoceros and snort. I could write a *Stutterer's Guide to Europe,* too: the titters in old Vienna, the knowing English remembering their King, the raw scorching baitings I met with in Greece, surrounded sometimes like a muzzled bear. The fourth means of effecting a cure I heard about was based on the fact that stutterers are able to sing without stuttering; hence, the victim should swing one of his arms like a big pendulum and talk in time to this—which again was obviously a worse fate than the impediment. Though I didn't try it, I was sent to a lady voice teacher who laid my hand on her conspicuous chest so that I could "feel her breathe." For just that moment the lessons worked wonderfully; if I wasn't speechless I spoke in a rush.

Stammering (a less obtrusive word I used to prefer)

127

apparently is not unattractive to women. It's a masculine encumbrance; five times as many men as women suffer from it. I was seldom alone while I was in Europe, and once or twice girls told me by way of a pick-me-up that they'd loved someone "for" his stutter. When I went into my seizures at parties, if a woman didn't step back she stepped forward, whereas the men did neither. The female instinct does not apply nearly so favorably to other afflictions. In our glib age the stutterer has even been considered a kind of contemporary hero, a presumed honest man who is unable to gab with the media people. Beyond the particular appeal of this image, it does seem to suit a writer. Publishers are fastidious types and some whom I've met have sidled away in distress from my flabbering face as soon as they could, but they probably remembered my name if they caught it. The purity image or Billy Budd stuff didn't intrigue them, just the hint of compulsion and complexity. Though I don't greatly go for either picture, in social terms I've thought of my stutter as a sort of miasma behind the Ivy League-looking exterior. People at parties take me for William Buckley until I begin, so I keep my mouth shut and smile prepossessingly just as long as I can.

Being in these vocal handcuffs made me a desperate, devoted writer at twenty. I worked like a dog, choosing each word. I wrote two full-length novels in iambic meter and a firehose style. Three hundred review copies of the second of these were sent out, but I received, I think, only three reviews. This was new pain, a man's career pain, with its attendant stomach trouble and neck and back cramps. A couple of years after that I got divorced from my first wife, and bawled like a half-butchered bull for an hour, rolled up on the floor of my apartment, while the two homosexuals next door listened in silence close to the wall, wondering what they ought to do. It was a purge, but the pain of that experience I remember best was an earlier scene. I'd announced to my wife, whom I loved and still love, my belief that we needed to separate. The next time we talked she crossed the room to my chair, knelt down beside me and asked what was going to become of each of us. That is the most painful splinter in my life, the most painful piece of the past. With variations the ache was prolonged through many fugitive suppers. In fact we still meet, holding hands and laughing at each other's jokes until we feel tears.

Who knows which qualities are godly? Pain probably makes us a bit godly, though, as tender love does. It makes us rue and summarize; it makes us bend and yield up ourselves. Pain is a watchdog medically, telling us when to consult a doctor, and then it's the true-blue dog at the bedside who rivals the relatives for fidelity. Last summer my father died of cancer. We had made peace, pretty much, a few years before. Although he had opposed my desire to be a writer, he ended up trying to write a book too, and he turned over to me at the last an old family history which he'd been hiding, partly because it mentioned a lot of muteness among my ancestors and partly in order to prevent my exploiting the stories. My voice and my liberal opinions grew a little more clarion in the household during the months he was dying. From a selfish standpoint, I suppose I was almost ready for him to die, but I was very earnestly sorry for every stage of rough handling involved in the process and for his own overriding regret that his life was cut off. Having lost our frank fear of death along with our faith in an afterlife, we have all adopted our fear of pain as a feeble alternative. Our regret, too, is magnified. When he was in discomfort I stuttered a great deal, but when he was not, when he was simply reminiscing or watching TV, I stuttered scarcely a bit. Then, as he was actually dying, during our last interview, he turned on the bed and asked me something. My answer was blocked in my mouth and his face went rigid with more pain than mine. He was startled because in the exigencies of dying he had forgotten that my infirmity was still there unhealed. He straightened, shutting his eyes, not wanting to end his life seeing it. Nevertheless, he'd often told me that it was my problems he loved me for rather than for my successes and sleekness. He loved my sister for being waiflike and my mother for being on occasion afraid she was mentally ill.

We were quite hardy while the months passed. Mother and he lay side by side on the bed clasping hands. Because of the pills, until nearly the end he was not suffering pain of the magnitude he had dreaded. The last couple of days there was a tossing, pitching, horrific pain, but the body more than the mind was responding—the body attempting to swallow its tongue. What I remember, therefore, of death's salutation to my father was that it came as a tickler, making his withered body twitch, touching him here and touching him there, wasting his tissues away like white wax, while his head on the headrest above looked down and watched; or he'd shoot an acute glance at me from out of the hunching amalgam of pricks, jactitation and drug-induced torpor. Death tickled him in a gradual crescendo, taking its time, and, with his ironic attorney's mind, he was amused. His two satisfactions were that he was privy to its most intimate preparations, everything just-so and fussy, and that at last the long spiky battling within the family was over and done. The new summer blossomed. In mid-June I saw what is meant by "a widow's tears." They flow in a flood of tremulous vulnerability, so that one thinks they will never stop.

Most severe on the physiologists' scale of pain is that of childbirth. It's also the worst that I've seen. A year had gone by since I'd left the Army and quit visiting my Philadelphia friend. She came to New York, looked me up, discovered me vomiting, thin as a rail because of girl trouble, and moved in with me on the Upper West Side, spooning in food and mothering me. Then, at about the time I perked up, she told me that she had got pregnant by a chap back in Philadelphia.

We drew out our savings and started for San Francisco, that vainglorious, clam-colored city. In her yellow convertible, with my English setter and her cocker spaniel, we drove through the South and through Texas, taking Highway 80 because it was the autumn and cold. I remember that whenever we stopped by the side of the road in Mississippi to let the dogs pee, and I shouted if one of them dawdled, any black woman or man who happened to be close by would turn to see what I wanted, quite naturally, as if I had called. It was a grueling trip. I'd begun vomiting again after my friend told me she was pregnant, and she was suffering mysterious pains in that region between her legs, which no druggist would touch. But we reached Russian Hill and established ourselves in one of the local apartment hotels. For a while during the seven-month wait this living arrangement didn't work out and she moved to a Florence Crittenton Home and I went to the beach, but we ended the period together. At six one morning I drove her up to a whelk-pink hospital on a breezy hill and sat in the labor room for eight hours, watching the blue grid of stretch marks on her anguished stomach: awful pain. She jolted and screamed, sucking gas from a cup, squeezing my hand and falling asleep between the throes. It took me three days to stop shaking, though it was a normal delivery throughout, and she, by the mental safety catch which women have, had blocked off most of the memory by the time she was wheeled to her room asleep. I'm ashamed to say that I'd spanked her a little the night before, not realizing it was the night before; I never spanked her again.

The contract she'd signed obliged my friend to re-linquish the baby girl to the Home for three weeks, after which she could appropriate her completely as her own. I was privileged to keep her breasts flowing during those weeks, a luxury that would have been fitting for Zeus; and, to the astonishment of the Home, as soon as the interval expired we showed up for the child. This was so rare that they wondered whether we were kidnappers. Then we drove East. The baby acquired a stepfather before she was out of her infancy and is now about ten.

So, pain is a packet of chiseling tools. Women in labor make no bones about protesting its severity. Neither does a dying man once he has stopped lingering with the living —thinking of the memories of his behavior which he is leaving his children, for instance. It's when we have no imperative purpose in front of our sufferings that we think about "bearing up"; "bearing up" is converted to serve as a purpose. Pain, love, boredom, and glee, and anticipation or anxiety—these are the pilings we build our lives from. In love we beget more love and in pain we beget more pain. Since we must like it or lump it, we like it. And why not, indeed?

THE LAPPING,
ITCHY EDGE
OF LOVE

We're to have a baby soon. I can feel him bang my wife's stomach, and already, even before he is born, we're losing sleep and discombobulated. During the night M. shifts in discomfort from the bed to the sofa and back, although her face is at a pitch of beauty much of the time, and occasionally we're seized with momentary panic that the event is now. Since we have not been married long, the pregnancy has brought us into an instant intimacy. We're hanging pictures and buying the furniture we hadn't bothered with earlier; a dozen times a day I nuzzle her—"Into the lion's mouth!" I say. Sometimes her belly seems very large, and that's a little alarming, but sometimes it seems to grow smaller and that's depressing. M. wears loose sweaters so that she can pull the neck open and look down the front, talking directly to him. I claim that he's a frog jumping under a towel, but she says his movements are like oatmeal slowly, irregularly bubbling—a cooking sensation—unless he stands painfully on her spleen. A girl in the prenatal class at the hospital startled the group by confessing she couldn't tell the difference between her baby's stirrings and gas. The instructor ignored this and returned to the subject of pushing: "Think vagina." Putting on diaper-like pads, the girls lay on their backs, opened their legs and practiced the exercise: push, push and blow; push, push and blow. "Push, Mrs. Winograd. You're not pushing."

Alone, we make babies of one another in preparation for the baby, or M. will poke her stomach sharply and look intently at it, as if she can see through inside. She pushes her stomach against me or lies on the couch wiggling her feet, but I tell her that she's too fat to kiss; I tell her the only reason she's still beautiful and hasn't turned from beauty into beast is that I've kissed her so much in the past.

This is my first baby, but not my first marriage. Both marriages began in neurotic confusion and a sense of impasse, though they were honest in the fact that love quickly grew. Usually people love because they want to; we love when we're ready to love, which, as often as not, is when we think we have reached a dead end. There is also that agitating wait for the chance meeting—the meeting some people wait for their whole lives long—but unless we're ready to marry we're not likely to, no matter whom we manage to meet. As we climb in and out of bedrooms and run to parties, we're partly ransacking ourselves for the potential to tarry awhile and not lose hope or lose our temper or our trust.

Since, at first, love includes such a dose of the urgencies, in the weeks before the wedding ceremony one comes back and comes back to see that this really *is* the right person and that the marriage isn't simply being jumped into because each of you feels boxed in. M.'s mother, a widow for many years, married again shortly before we did, so she and her mother were mirroring one another's emotions. For my part, I'd thought ever since my divorce that I'd thrown my first marriage away carelessly, arrogantly, ignorantly, and so I'd been eagerly awaiting my chance to try again. That had been the blundering marriage of one's twenties; this was the marriage of which much is hoped.

On our wedding morning we spoke over the phone on tiptoe, not wanting to upset anything. Then the happiness, the confidence, the chatter afterwards—*at last*—and the exuberance of the word "wife." I knew I was giving myself more wholeheartedly than before, with less wariness and self-distrust. I'd had four years of bachelorhood between marriages and was sick of it: I realized again how sick when I went on a business trip for several weeks, returning unexpectedly, and found the apartment a mess: earrings on the floor, dust in puffs, tumbled clothes. I'm a neatness bug, but this disorder just seemed like delicious complexity.

We had a short, auspicious honeymoon, with Edwardian meals, champagne, flowers, and strolls in the park, where I talked through the bars to the Bengal tigers in their own language by way of indicating my competence as a bridegroom. Now we own a wine-red Parego baby

136

carriage and wait for the sea change which is under way. It's a peculiarly vulnerable juncture, like the month before one goes into the Army, when every hearty soul who has preceded you is an authority on what you ought to expect. The natural-childbirth people speak of the penultimate pleasure which their program of yoga builds up to, while in the opposite camp are the jumpy ladies who confide to M. that labor is brutal beyond describing. Most people do neither; they simply say by the light in their faces that the childbearing years are about as gay as any they can remember. We're told, incidentally, that our Jeremy (as we think of him) is going to be a girl, because the heartbeat is strong and steady and the outline of M.'s stomach is generally round, not humpy, although as big as a pumpkin.

For the time being the preludes of sex bore me—the whole repetitive preoccupation with the next pair of bobbledeboobs. It's probably part of the conditioning for fatherhood, but it should enable me to set down some erotica without wetting the page. Of course everything is fluids—kissing is fluids, babies are fluids, having a baby is fluids. Thank God a shapeless being is going to emerge instead of somebody already formed—a little loan shark or a beauty queen. In the pudginess is a new beginning. One girl I know has relegated sex to oblivion by another means. She is in residence at a famous group-therapy center on the West Coast where hugging is the path to the godhead, and she pays her way by giving massages, herself naked. I can see her among her customers, all of them male, because she's a peachy-cheeked, moist-lipped girl, tall, big-figured and energetic, always a searcher, always in earnest, and rather chaste. The week her divorce became final she cut off her hair, but she may have grown it out again. I see her struggling with the bodily cholers of the man of the hour, who now over-, now under-reacts. At this center the patient is encouraged to holler. It hurts him a bit, but the obstructive ego is gradually dislodged.

As a boy I too was taught to try to cut down on my self-centeredness, though the method was merely for me to try to reduce my use of the pronoun "I." When I wrote home from camp I would scan the letter, notice how often "I" occurred, and cross it out wherever I could, changing the sentence structure or implying the word. We're all told to be less selfish, that we must love as well as be loved, but I was slow. After a late entry into the world of sex, it was my satisfaction during my twenties to see a brief succession of girls fall into involvements with me. I watched and did my best to help it happen and then, like a kindly pasha, would try to make it easy for them. Only after the fact did the sensations of love or despair or scrupulous empathy penetrate me.

Madness is the main fear we have nowadays, and even ahead of the immediacies of love, my relations with women have been full of apprehensiveness on this score: fear that my mother was going crazy, fear of derangement in my first wife, and in my second, though much less so. If I've not cared for a woman, I've still managed to wonder once in a while whether she was going nuts; I just haven't been as rattled by the possibility. None of my dire premonitions has ever come true, and, needless to say, I've doubted my own mind as well; but the sterility of being engrossed this way makes my thirty-some years seem years of skimming—a bumbling, problematical passage which, while it has taken a long time to live, sometimes appears more like a rehearsal for life than a life actually being lived. Even sexually it seems to me I am inexperienced, because there is a deadly sameness to my history: accepting love as soon as it's offered, growing very exacting and bossy, but later in a curious turnabout becoming submissive and boylike, a sort of "mother's helper," as one girl put it, until the affair reached its indifferent end, whereupon I could exercise my talent for tender regret.

I think that most people feel inexperienced in love and sex. Either they've loved only one woman and wistfully envy the mustachioed philanderer, or else they've philandered themselves and wish that they'd been deep and true. How the world admires the staunch old fellow who has seen his wife through thick and thin, raised his family, and never once looked to the side. But how it cherishes the old reprobate too—the rake of seventy-three who still has a gleam in his eye, who loved 'em up and wet his wick and left 'em high and dry! Most of us can admit that we started off pretty well, with a doting father and hovering mother, but we fouled up that nest in short order: it wasn't fitting that we just love them; we had to defy them and shake them off too. Then, having been stand-offish in one set of circumstances, it's not so easy to stop. So you look back and see yourself, a suggestible, quite consistent figure of fun, through the succession of old neighborhoods and changing cities and combinations and pairings of friends and various institutional arrangements and tie-ins, and it's as if all along you had been expecting the chance for a second run-through—as if you've been rehearsing. In the resignation that masquerades as cynicism, perhaps, or in a sense of confident, fortified quietude, you can recognize the distinctions between now and when you were "young"; nevertheless, you still do feel young and blundering. The figure you've cut remains about the same as far back as you can remember: piling minor mistake upon minor mistake, in fairly good faith, never eminent, never in jail, but leading, however adventurously, a quite uneventful life.

All three proposals of marriage I've made were prompted, not volunteered: once when the girl was already spoken for, once by an impatient brother-in-law, and once by the fact of conception. Pregnancy is not a bad reason for getting married, it seems to me, since there are other options, in any case, and the period provides a quick testing in loyalty and cooperation. We quarreled in order to pull on the ties binding us, and then from the same intuitive, compelling affinity which had drawn us into the fix, we decided gaily to go ahead. More than gaily; we decided the fix was the jackpot. The wedding was followed by a month of baby-talk. You can't quarrel in baby-talk, and of course by now we didn't want to quarrel. On the one hand, it was too late, and on the other it was too early. Quarreling only suits an established marriage. Both of us having marinated in bachelorhood long enough, an established marriage was what we wanted. In courtship you worry and wriggle towards the edge of love, and we knew ourselves to have reached the edge.

Our first child will arrive a few months before my fourth book is published, since I am tardy in these matters. I was a virgin when the first book came out; indeed, I hoped that being published would help me with girls. It didn't, but a gathering aura of neediness did. I'd been afraid I was homosexual, though I'd done nothing overt since the ninth grade, when a friend and I made lip-smacking noises in the dark at a party after our more advanced friends, who had brought girls, turned out the lights at 11 P.M. We sat awkwardly on each other's laps; and for years afterwards I did now and then feel the impulse to embrace a man, until the hubbub of heterosexual sex submerged it. For one thing, I liked breasts too much to become a faggot. I wanted the breast so much that I couldn't believe that a woman might want me to have it too. The word "modesty," which was the word I heard used, should have given the secret away, since you are often modest about what you are rather proud of.

Already in grammar school a white blouse was exciting when worn by a black-haired girl. I couldn't make the first move, but when I got home from school the baby-sitter who looked after my sister would tell me to stretch out on the couch with my head in her lap. Even this invitation embarrassed me, and usually I'd eat a big bowl of cornflakes instead and turn on *Jack Armstrong*.

141

When I was fourteen I got to know the town veterinarian because of his interest in falconry. He was no great shakes as a vet, so I had steered clear of him with my dogs, but he trapped duck hawks every spring on the flyway which passed over Oenoke Ridge, and starved them in hoods and trained them and sneaked out stealthily at night to the spacious brown barns at Hoyt's Nurseries to catch the wild pigeons which roosted there and were an acceptable meal. His wife was a French war bride with a white startled face. They stayed late in bed in the morning, and when he appeared he was always yawning. The yawn is what I remember about him, more than the shed full of hawks. Without really knowing what it meant, I imitated him, and on some subterranean level I still seem to like the picture of myself yawning.

Then there were the maids we had, a series of Negro and old Polish ladies. As a small boy I was fascinated by their poverty and poor education but not until later did I realize that they were as female as anyone else. They didn't figure in my daydreams; the dream girls were blondies who lived in the forest and needed an outlaw protector like me. I masturbated oddly anyway. As a Boy Scout trainee, I had read in the Manual about "Conservation," which equated strewing one's spunk on the bedsheets with burning down woods and polluting streams, so I used to keep the stuff in, pressing my finger on the duct until the contractions stopped. Later on, like everyone else, when I let it out, I would pull back the covers to see how far up the bed it had shot.

While one is a youngster watching others make out,

bachelorhood is not the inert sort of interval that it becomes. The shoeleather I beat to death! I walked and walked, looking at lights across the Hudson, the Allegheny, the Mississippi. Every lonely lighted window in the distance seemed to mark where a woman sat by herself, though the excitement of seeing the wide world was sufficient for me without pushing my luck and trying to meet someone. I hung around the burlesque halls, however, astonished whenever the dancers spoke from the stage, endowing their public bodies with the squeaky voice of a piglet squeezed. In several experiences with prostitutes I was impotent. They were my neighbors in the hotels where I was staying, so we were friendly later, but in Chicago I went to a roaring six-story whorehouse with a special exit into a dogleg alley, everyone blacker than I was used to, and I was scared. The woman's room was equipped like a midwife's except that it was painted red; she was fortyish and had a pup underneath the bed which at first I imagined to be a mugger; the building echoed like a pocket Algiers. My chums in Times Square had asked me whether their being black was what hung me up, but this woman didn't; she just said to go ahead and do to her anything I could think of. When I couldn't think of anything, she pushed a wallet-like breast out of her brassiere in exactly the spirit I had expected a woman would have if I'd let her know how I coveted her breasts: oh, if *that's* what you want.

The first girl I really went out with had a better-shaped back than front, as a matter of fact; it was a marvelously graceful back. My feet smelled terrible that year—it's an ailment the nervous suffer from—they smelled like a forest fire. Her father would ask if a tire was burning somewhere in the house, and I'd go upstairs and run the tub or sit with my feet on the window sill or suggest going out for a walk. It seems as though all we ever did was walk. Finally I did lose my cherry, and discovered, among other revelations, that I could talk to women with less difficulty than I had with men. At college when I'd walked about Cambridge with a mountain climber named Pamela I'd been unable to muster a single comment except that the houses were "strange," or such and such a professor was "strange," because "strange" was the only word I could get out. We lay at the foot of the Bunker Hill Monument, so that it loomed like a giddy cliff over us, the spotlight on it, and hitchhiked chastely across Massachusetts, always like mutes, never exchanging a word. But now the magical greasing powers of sex, of touch, had unblocked my mouth, and I held forth with all of the eloquence of a prisoner released. Of course it did me no harm with my new friend that I continued to stutter badly with everyone else, because she assumed that this was explicit proof of love. I suppose for a minute or two sometimes it was. A hasty trotting period followed, spent in basement apartments that smelled of cats. I went on ersatz honeymoons in New Hampshire with heavy German girls and lady writers, their short stories waiting unread at the *Partisan Review* going on ten months. At this point also I fell for the future wife of a close friend; there was a guilty chest-beating to-do on my part about that. Apparently she thinks that my infatuation was permanent,

144

and there aren't many irritations to match the condescension which a woman metes out to a man who she believes has loved her vainly for the past umpteen years.

My first wife was a mathematician who was living in the Bronx in half of a subway motorman's house. Van Cortlandt Park was close, and Sugar Ray Robinson lived nearby. I was writing a prizefight book, so I watched his house, which was equipped with blinking tree lights and broken pugilists who served as houseboys. I had a motor scooter and combat boots, and when my first wife heard their crunch along the sidewalk she knew that it was either me or a murderer. Mr. Clean, the detergent man, with a ring in one ear and a shaved head, was another neighborhood celebrity. In retrospect the whole courtship has a poignancy because of her earnestness and because of details of this sort, just the kind that old-marrieds recite. She is somebody I'll never meet in anyone else's skin, and when we last talked on the phone I twisted and throbbed and couldn't speak, though I was capricious and domineering as a husband, faithful only in a literal sense. We lived in howling cold tenements because if anybody was living that way in the pomp of New York we wanted to too; I was the radical and she was the idealist. But for half our time together we traveled to Sicily and Spain, needing to lean on each other wherever we were because of being strangers, and hence procrastinating on our central problems. Oddly enough, timid as I was, I was a father in that marriage instead of a son, and while I made some redeeming gestures, my memories of my behavior are mostly of the obstinacies, petty and large. In particular, I wouldn't let her have a child, which is a sore thought in this present gleeful interlude because it bewildered her and made her wretched. It was the sticking point; it was what I withheld. Later I offered her the child, under whatever circumstances, and turned on the waterworks. She was the strong one then, though while we were married it didn't seem she was going to be. To try to describe her—her voice, her dresses, her squirrel's-nest hair, the way she walked and wore her high collars— is fruitless and painful. Later I cried, later I loved, when it was too late. There were reunions and pinpoint depictions of the whole-cake, whole-spirited love that we had hoped in our clearest moments to achieve. Finally we got the divorce, printed in Spanish, which rests in my safe deposit box—that dreary receptacle—along with a yellowing christening certificate, my father's will, and several repudiated contracts and unlucky investments. Young as we were, constituted as we were, and given the jazzy climate of divorce of the period, we did what we did, smashing what we smashed. Although my new marriage casts a wider net and is serene by comparison, this early one remains like a rip in my life.

We begin, way back, with our mothers, and if a marriage breaks up we find to our astonishment that they are still there. Mine, when she heard a divorce had been decided upon, felt for a minute or two undivided delight: I was going to be hers. Instead, I put more distance between us. I was like the fellow I saw yesterday on the Gansevoort Pier sitting by the water on a copy of the *Sunday Times*. He had grown a fluff of hair on his lip to hide his fretting, he was balding, and he appeared miserable, though well under control, as a man old enough to be balding generally is. Rightly or not, I had the sense that he was depending on the bulky *Times* to hold him in place; at least reading it would kill a few hours. I was more fortunate; I went to Europe and began the wild-oats bachelorhood we are all eager for at one point or another.

All five girls from that year in Europe have turned up in New York recently: among them, the movie press agent's secretary who misused me slightly in Rome, the lanky Norwegian girl whom I rather misused, and the British girl whom I lived with in marital amity for a number of months. The two of us took up residence on Samos, and every evening we walked to the harbor to watch the caiques bob in the dusk, eat slices of octopus with a toothpick, and drink ouzo. We climbed to Zoodochos Pighi, a high monastery in the pine trees which is like a stone castle facing the Turkish mountain of Mycale. In France I knew a tough, rich American girl who loved to fight, whose eyes used to snap, as the saying goes, who tore into a fight with real relish, a marvelously brassy sexpot without the slightest socialist guilt about being so rich—she just liked the freedom and the purchasing power. We were appreciative of each other's bodies, and she was of the type who are writers' girls, who like raunching about with writers. At one time she had been married to a novelist who drank as the novelists of legend do and waved a pistol when he fought with her.

The first of the five to return was a frizzy-headed young redhead who had thought she loved me over there, but quickly realized she didn't when she got back to Manhattan. Though she was a persistent virgin, she used to let me take her into my bedroom and feel her bosom—which amounted to practically a third of her body because she was so skinny—while she watched my antics quietly, smiling a little. Then after a few minutes she'd leave (having interrupted a taxi ride, perhaps, in order to do this), with a show of affection on both sides but no reference to when we might see each other for longer. I suppose in her fundamentalist's way she was watching and waiting to see if I wouldn't fall for her head over heels, until she realized that she didn't care if I did. Her intensity was her greatest appeal—those blazing cheeks and half-shut eyes—but like a country girl come to the fair, she stood on her guard against malarkey.

I was a glutton for fannies, large mouths, and the other staples. Short-haired girls are sexy because their hair is short and long-haired girls are sexy because they're long-haired. The running around isn't really the same as onanism, because it's celebrative as onanism never is; but it surely is brusque. For one skittery long-haired research assistant, sexual intercourse was the "center" of every day; she thought she needed it that often. I didn't, but I got tired of the attempt before the idea. Her voice was like a bicycle horn and she thought my views on any subject were ridiculous; yet she had a soft spot for me and let me indulge my passion for her, which was carnal and virtually irremediable. I was always ringing her street bell, and she'd come out and kiss me, even if she had other company. Occasionally she may have hoped we would wind up married; she'd bring out slipcover fabrics for me to pass judgment on. We watched television in bed, heaped round domestically with blankets because it was a drafty Village apartment with warped floorboards. Her closets were stuffed with clothes I didn't like, but we went in for nudity a good deal. Her bathroom was painted black and red and heavily scented; a whole wall of the apartment was hung with beads and belts. Since she got up early to go to work, I lay alone in the bed an extra hour, drinking in the smells, and feeling kept. When she was dressed she looked elfin, but she wasn't elfin undressed: I ate my way around her, and called and called and called, getting her infernal answering service or letting the phone ring thirty-five times. Sometimes I started out for her apartment if there was no answer so that I could at least anticipate arriving and trying the door. She had areolae the color of reddish acorns, a puffy stiff muff, a funny pad of fat just above her buttocks, and hair I trembled to take down when she asked in a beeping voice, "Would you undo my hair?"

As I say, the memory is of a twitchy frenzy, a zaftig, olive-country body one size larger than small, and lots of trekking back and forth between my house and hers. My balls felt like a bushel basket, and though she would have made my life a misery if we had married, a penis is like Steinbeck's Lenny—he doesn't know what's going on.

Let's see . . . These anecdotes are not about love, only about the itching.

On the East Side I knew a splendid neurotic blonde who owned more books than a bookstore and kept a cupboard full of hors d'oeuvres fixings and draped tapestries across her walls. She had a father problem and used to try to murder me with her big boobs—a flirt with death, as it were. "Don't smother; don't smother," she'd whisper, bearing down, stopping up my mouth and flattening my nose. She was another writers' girl; numerous colleagues of mine had borrowed money from her and disported themselves. She was breezy, friendly company, good for the eyes, and always danced away from commitment with a throaty chuckle. Now she's on the razor's edge of spinsterhood, while an understanding of her difficulties has begun to dawn on her; I suppose it's a race against time.

I knew a girl from Queens who lived in Brooklyn and was a barmaid in Manhattan. Later a Negro moved in with her, so that I couldn't talk to her when I phoned, but for a while she'd told me the adventures that came her way each night: men offering $20 just for a surreptitious squeeze. Ginny, my one youngster, a Wellesley senior, was another girl whose bosom was a cross she had to bear (her words). It wasn't so much for her bosom that I liked her, though, as for her sunny nature, her intelligence, her sturdy bottom and her fine-textured yellow hair. She was a round-faced, classy beauty, plump, smooth-skinned, brown-eyed, and all the other things we love. Not to leave her as perfection, she had an asthmatic's pigeon-ridge marring her chest, and she had father troubles too, the fellow having allowed his boss to assault her in exchange for a promotion, so that when she came near a high window, she would muse about ending it all. But she was born to thrive, it seemed to me; she was joyful, and I enjoyed the tutor's role, showing her that she had gifts to give, that she could put a man to sleep when no pill could—that she was practically all gifts, indeed. She had fun experimenting with me in such activities as quarreling and letter-writing, until she graduated from college and went to Bonn to work for a newsmagazine.

There are the girls you hold your breath for because their breath is bad; there are the stringbean spirited girls who entwine you in every move they make because they squirm so much; there are the generous-hearted, squared-off girls—daughters of butchers' union organizers, who served time in the WACs, perhaps—who are around to talk to. My address book still has a currency because the phone numbers are up-to-date, and a married man without such a recent acquaintance with the bleaker winds of bachelorhood might feel that he was missing out somehow, reading about the new morality, the lurid teenie-boppers. As a heterosexual, half the world is potentially his lover; half the world seems to be bending its primary energies to attract him, and sometimes it must be a little painful when he walks in the evening streets.

Dealing with people is a question of finding out what is important to them, but we seldom bothered to. The anonymity, the state of war, the rush, the risks, the tantalizing, the pounding uptown and down: these made the prize seem like a prize. Once every year or two I was meeting a girl I might have married with a fair prospect for success, and we would pretend that it was coming true, that we had somebody to bring our bruises to, somebody to live with. Actually it was the brink of love, but I would make the simulation do, quite content to pretend that we were married or soon to be so. When the liaison fell through I'd change apartments or take some time out for despair. Once I sent some of my friends an invitation to my own funeral: which is the craziest thing I've done.

So finally with M. the vigilance relaxed, the canniness. Like an exhausted manatee, I sighed and sank down, letting myself cross the brink. So did she, for that matter, whose history in these proceedings had been similar to mine, when you boil it down. We got ourselves pregnant more by inner design than by coincidence, and now she wanders around the apartment in the middle of the night, eating Mallomars and figs, while we wait for this hollering orange to make an appearance, this Molly-Jeremy. We already have love enough to extend to the baby, but no baby as yet, so we play endless naming games, and M. pokes me exploratively with her thumb. You can't fall out of loving a baby; you can't divorce a baby. And we look backwards at our parents. M.'s father, an articulate, turbulent man, used to enter the room where she was doing her homework and lift her glasses off, clean them for her, and give them back, going out again without a word. Although, in company with one-third of American men, I thought my mother's love verged on a passion, when she phones now it is mainly because she is alone, is a widow and must face the empty house. She's a graceful, likable woman, Western and tall, and I must shake off my habit of shaking her off.

152

VIOLENCE,
VIOLENCE

It is curious that with such a crushing, befuddling climate of general violence as there is in New York we should still be paying money to go to the prizefights. The fight fan, as one used to picture him, was a kind of overweight frustrated homebody whose life was practically devoid of danger and drama. Middle-aged rather than young, a small businessman or a warehouse foreman, a nostalgic war veteran, he looked about and found the world torpid, so he came to St. Nicholas Arena to holler and twist on his folding chair, throw starts of punches, or did the same thing in front of the television set in a bar. But now this fellow has all the firepower of Vietnam on television, the racial-college riots, the hippies to hate, the burglaries in his building, the fear of being mugged when he is on the street. Going home from the prizefight, he runs a chance of being beaten up worse than the loser was. And boxing, which began as an all-out sport, has not been able to cinch its procedures tighter, the way pro football has, to make for a more modish, highstrung commotion and wilder deeds. It's the simplest pageant of all: two men fight, rest a minute, and fight some more. Like the mile run, it's traditionalist and finite, humble in its claims.

Baseball, which seemed the natural man's sport above all, has turned out to be overly ceremonious and time-consuming for the 1960s, and even burlesque and the belly dancers of Eighth Avenue, forthright as we once supposed they were, have been eclipsed by still more elementary displays of the human physique. The entre-preneurs of boxing didn't at first suspect that their sport had any kick left except as a TV filler for the hinter-lands, where the old modes prevail. The custom of weekly fights at St. Nick's or the old Garden had lapsed (since which, both buildings have gone *poof*). But then they tried a few cards at the National Maritime Union hiring hall, counting on the roughhouse seamen to provide a box-office backlog. When the shows sold out, they shifted them to the Felt Forum in the new Madison Square Garden and discovered that the sport pays there as well. As a result, live boxing has become a feature of New York life again. The problem of the promoters is not to stream-line the *Geist* to fit the sixties but to find fighters who fight, because unlike many other athletes, prizefighters do not really enjoy their sport very much, as a rule; they fight for the purse. All our Irish and Italian citizens have elevated themselves until they don't have to choose be-tween simonizing cars for a living or the prize ring, and the Negroes and Spanish-speakers too are scrambling upward toward better livelihoods, if only in campier sports with lots of legwork, or the various ornate sports where if the team loses the coach loses his job. Boxing isn't like that, and we are bringing in hungry souls from Nigeria, the Philippines and the Bahamas to do the dirt. People sometimes make the mistake of feeling sorry for boxers, however, and want to abolish the sport, when they should look instead at the man in the neighborhood car wash who *isn't* a fighter—doesn't fly to Seattle for a big card —but runs the steam hose and polishes fenders.

And is it dirt? I'm not one of those professional eye-witnesses who is willing to watch anything just on the grounds that it is happening. I live on Ambulance Alley and don't need to go to the Garden in order to see men in desperate straits. I go to admire a trial of skills, a contest of limited violence between unintimidated adversaries which, even when it does spill out of the ring after a bad decision and the crowd in its anger sways shoulder to shoulder, is very nineteenth-century, from the era of cart horses in the street. Every sport is a combat between its participants, but boxing is combat distilled, purer even than combat with weapons. When a referee steps in and stops a fight in which one man is receiving punishment without any hope of recouping, the crowd is not disappointed at seeing the punishment stopped; they are glad enough about that. If they are disappointed, it's because the drama is over, which was true as soon as the fight became one-sided. Boxing's appeal is its drama and grace, a blizzarding grace that amounts to an impromptu, exigent ballet, especially in the lighter and

155

nimbler weights. Hands, arms, feet, legs, head, torso—
more is done per moment than in fast ice hockey; and
since there is more motion, the athletes in other sports
cannot surpass a consummate boxer for grace.

Still, why this extra violence in such a violent time?
Is it choreographed like a bullfight; is it like a fine
tragedy which one goes to although one's own life is
tangled enough? Of course it isn't these things at all.
There is no program, no unity, no meaning as such unless a parable fortuitously develops, and the spectators
are there for the combat. Writers of the Hemingway-
Mailer axis have been fascinated by the combat, locating
relevancies and identities in the pre-fight rituals, but they
have not made claims for the sport as an art. Ten years
ago, when we did not live alongside such an ocean of
violence, some of us went to the fights perhaps as one
keeps an aquarium. We realized most of the world was
under water, but we were high and dry with Eisenhower,
and knowing that life is salt and life is action, life is
tears and life is water, we kept a fish tank to represent
the four-fifths of the world which breathed with gills.

But nowadays we're flooded and swimming for dear
life, no matter where we happen to live. That we nevertheless prefer our sports violent—the irreducible concise-
ness of boxing—is evidence of a relation to violence, a
need and a curiosity, so basic that it cannot be sated.
Though we do tire of the delirium in the streets, we are
only tiring of the disorder. Make it concise, put ropes or
white lines around it, and we will go, we will go, just as
people on vacation go down to the roaring sea.

BLITZES
AND HOLDING
ACTIONS

Every October the cowboys used to come to town for the rodeo at Madison Square Garden, and if you frequented certain obscure hotels (the Washington and Jefferson on West 51st Street was one), you could see them killing time in the lobby, their spurs tinkling softly as they moved to the soft-drink machine and the magazine stand. Both cowboy and Indian getups have come into fashion lately, as part of the substitution of shadow for substance which has grown general in the U. S. (though at least the hippies and homosexuals who dress Western do frankly find the shadow more intriguing than they do the facts—shadow piled upon shadow as a sort of art form). But all one's enthusiasms of years ago have had fads catch up with them—soul music, which used to ring out from the nether ends of the radio dial, and jogging and mountain climbing and professional football. The speed at which new diversions must be discovered brings us the freedom or *hubris* of today, which is to range back and forth across the centuries and wear Roman togas, if we like, or play ruffled fop of the Restoration, jog like a hunting bushman, practice ancient love-making arts with tongue and dildo, riot for bread and peace in the streets, play eunuchs-and-Amazons, send out space men, develop robots, and train our shock troops in the crafts of Thuggee.

All this made it seem salubrious that a "festival" rodeo was booked for the Garden last week. Cowboys aren't figures as fundamental to the American past as lumberjacks are (now there's an enthusiasm that hasn't gone public!), but like the lumberjacks, they preceded the farmers and traveling salesmen across the continent wherever the terrain permitted, by a matter of decades sometimes, and the farmer, dodging his bull and hectoring his chickens, and the traveling salesman, grinding his gears and bullying his car, each thought of himself as a secret cowboy. Then the writers got into it; a cat can look at a king, but a cat who can go to the movies can become a king. Of course a rodeo cowboy is not the same thing as a regular cowboy. His injuries are legion and legendary, and since he earns only his winnings, he must win or starve—a raw arrangement that the frontier itself couldn't top. In regard to the animals, his concern is not their welfare or poundage but rather the seconds elapsing while he performs such fetishized feats as calf roping which have been lifted out of the working cowboy's rigamarole year. Wild-cow-milking makes a stunt out of a hungry man's gambit. Brahma-bull-riding is plain nouveau thrill, because it has no basis in the events on a ranch; it's a wrinkle on breaking broncs, having nothing to do with the work at hand, so that the rodeo cowboy becomes like the driver racing at Le Mans.

This is not to belittle the sport, only to emphasize that it is a sport, technicalized and professionalized with an eye to the box office; it's a living and a career. It is also a penultimate bauble of Americana with a heroic history yet a busy present, and I've often thought about investigating it in detail. Whenever a rodeo arrives in town I look forward to going, but after I get there I am somewhat repelled by the superfluous brutality—superfluous to good livestock management, anyway, if not to the requirements of a slam-bang sport purporting to represent the frontier. It's as if one of the teams in a football game were not a highly paid group of glamor guys but were slave gladiators whose job was to put up a stubborn resistance while being beaten limp. As a boy I sneaked through the stage entrance of the Boston Garden several times to look at the animals after the show, and I saw them in Colorado also. They did indeed resemble a team of a kind, bushed and cowed and wrung dry, standing thirstily by the water trough in a bunch, making no distinctions as to which was which—the broncs, the bulls, the calves and the steers, who were shaking their aching necks, all facing me, jumbled together like animals after a forest fire. They lunged in panicky reflex when the caretaker cowboys approached, and their panic, operating with the handlers' own tiredness and exasperation, complicated the process of bedding them down; hats, whips and fists were thrown until

159

it was painful to watch. Then they stood in their pens, panting and stupefied, as if a forest fire had passed and left them alive. Once, in a moment of sympathy, one of the cowboys stopped and said with a smile to a horse, "No speak English?"

Writers can be categorized by many criteria, one of which is whether they prefer subject matter that they rejoice in or subject matter they deplore and wish to savage with ironies. Since I'm of the first type, these mixed feelings of mine about rodeos keep me eagerly coming and then backing up. The cowboys, too, back away. The falls they absorb, the cracked clavicles, the pounding 500-mile overnight drives between shows—all part of the life—turn them to thinking about that little cottonwood ranch somewhere that they want to buy when their winnings rise, where they need only yell Yowee from the door of the barn once or twice to bring the cattle on the run to be fed.

I notice the midnight cowboys don't go to the rodeo much; it's mostly the boots and the hats that they're interested in. Nor do my several writer friends who write shoot-em-ups—the gunfire West appeals to them. I'm a merry-go-round fan, however. I watch for at least a few minutes whenever I pass a merry-go-round. There is a milling surge, a herd seethe—the machinery whirs like the horses' hooves and the windy calliope beats as bravely as the horses' lungs. How high you go, and how low: an inch seems a foot. Looking back, you see the lunging jam of horses behind, with their jaws turned up, their snaking necks, and the force of a tide lifting them on.

From the side rail, the thrash and the bite and the blurring surge are even better; I can watch headily for two hours, as if some epochal life-drive were being reenacted —geese going north or a salmon run. The motion has a round-and-round structure that makes for perfection, nothing on earth being so close to perfect as a circle. And of course the real triumphs of a carousel are, first, that it seems natural—small pinto horses catapulting— and second, that it is the only place in the city where, day in and day out, every face aboard is young and alight.

So I come to the rodeo eager for the round-and-round monotony of the arena, which concentrates the spectator on the exploits of the cowboys better than any straightaway could ("rodeo" means to go around, in fact). Since they can't go anywhere, they only *ride;* nothing steals the scene. And they really *do* ride, because they are graded on the horse's performance as well as their own. If the horse or the bull or whatever doesn't perform, the rider loses the event. He must maximize the spunk left in his animal, make him make it a close contest, as in a bullfight. He blitzes the bronc and *holds* the steer.

Sadly enough, the National Mexican Festival and Rodeo, which is what the management of the new Garden has begun signing up each October by way of a rodeo, is not a rodeo. It's a tidy little package production which presents Antonio Aguilar, a Mexican recording star and feature of 103 movies, and his wife and eight-year-old son, singing a great many protracted songs and prancing on Portuguese high-school horses. Aguilar is a personable man, a topnotch horseman, and his voice is better than Roy Rogers' was; he too sings, "Oh, give me a home"; and his show rather suits the wheel of tiered spotlights and the sanitized atmosphere of the new Madison Square Garden—in the Spanish tradition, he kneels to the applause. He has a tense, springy mare, a leggy comic gelding, and there is some fine Roman riding, some fire-jumping and an all-girl drill. Four or five broncos are busted briefly in exhibitions during the intervals; also three or four big scared bulls. The Mexican lariat wizards make butterflies, flowers and ocean breakers with their *reatas*. But mainly the show is fancy dressage in lavender lighting. Arthur Godfrey, who sat in front of me, was pleased, being something of an expert on dressage. "Beautiful, beautiful," he kept saying. And the kids behind shouted to Antonio Aguilar, "Screw the horses, man. Just keep the grass coming through!" I wasn't opposed to it all. I just wished that since apparently, for whatever reasons, cowboys continue to mean a good deal to Americans, we could have a real rodeo in New York once a year.

THE MOOSE
ON THE WALL

Since it is likely that the last wild animals of large size and dignity that people will see will be stuffed ones, I paid a visit to my neighborhood taxidermist in northern Vermont to learn how he does his work, and what precisely it is: by what means these few crick-necked and powdery phantoms of the great game confluxes of the past will be preserved. The area where I live still has a smattering of black bear, and plenty of deer, some bobcats, and an occasional coyote migrating in from westerly parts. The beaver are beginning to come back, now that nobody traps them, and the groundhogs and skunks and porcupines are flourishing as the farms become summer places, where they aren't shot as varmints. The moose, cougar, wolves and wolverines are long gone, but the humbler animals, meek, elusive, adaptable, are doing all right for the moment—in fact, my friend the taxidermist says that when he was a boy and this was farm country, people would travel for miles just to set eyes on a bear's track, if one was reported. The wildlife left will probably continue to prosper until the seasonal owners break up their properties into smaller and smaller tracts as land values rise.

My friend is a likable man with white hair, a quiet, spacious, mild face well used by his sixty years, a farmer's suspenders, a carpenter's arms, and an acumen in the woods, or a love for the woods, that no doubt exceeds my own, though my bias and his are opposed. We are allies nevertheless, because hunting and nonhunting naturalists when taken together are only a dot in the populace, at least when wildlife conservation is involved. Clean air and water, provision for beaches and lakes and parks—these causes draw a dependable measure of support from good men everywhere, but animals unseen, whose wish is to steer clear of mankind, get less attention. Hunters do fret about them, however, keeping tabs on the toll the winter snows take, and the relentless shrinkage of open land. Hunters miss the moose and mountain lions and pass along rumors that a handful still somehow survive here in the Northeast. Besides, hunters are folk who like to walk half-a-dozen miles before having lunch, to get their feet wet, pant up the ledges and draws, cook over a fire, and perhaps finally haul a load of meat home on their backs; and they take their ration of blood as they find it, in a natural fashion, not transmogrified onto the TV. Hunters are as attentive as the predator animals to the habits of what they are after; and some of them want visible proof on the wall of what

164

they got for their trouble—the taxidermist does this for them. In some ways his work resembles an undertaker's, with the congenial difference that he needn't hurry or pretend to be sad.

In the window of his shop is an old display of two newborn bear cubs, bleached white by the sun, sitting in a tiny boat on a pond. The pond is represented by a sheet of plastic, with realistic-looking trout underneath. There are also some dusty pheasants and ducks, their colors dead now. But the splendor inside is undeniable— deep, virile black hides of bears seized at the prime, just before they would have dug in for a winter's sleep. These are stacked in piles, glossy, blue-black, and there are other mounds of orange and caribou-colored deer hides. Visiting, I was surprised at the number of tools along the workbench: fleshing and cartilage knives, saws and scalpels in rows, pliers, pincers, hammers and mallets, bone snippers and scrapers, curved sewing needles, forceps, punches, drills, picking tools, tweezers, stiff wires. The plywood tables are big enough for him to stretch out a nine-foot skin to dry after it has been soaked in the tanning tub and washed in fresh water. The soaking goes on for six weeks or so—he has sacks of alum, which is the main ingredient in the pickling acid. There is salt in quantity too, for drying the flesh side of the skins when they first arrive, and plaster of Paris, and sacks of a grainy roof-insulation material which is used to thicken the plaster of Paris.

Ideally, the taxidermist is given the skull of the animal along with the hide, if a head job is wanted, not simply the flat tanned skin. After boiling the skull until all the meat has fallen away, he rebuilds the original shape of the head by thumbing plaster into the grooves and cavities on the skull so that the skin fits over it again as neatly as before. For deer, whose jaws and teeth are not to be emphasized, he doesn't need more than the skull's top plate, where the antlers attach, but a carnivore is most realistically mounted when the teeth that you see are the real teeth, not hoked up from wax in an oversized jaw. He restructures the underpart of a deer's face by whittling a small block of cedar or basswood, though of course he could buy entire preformed heads made of papier mâché from the wholesalers—heads of moose, deer, or the numerous and various African antelopes. A ready-made jaguar's wax mouth and paper skull costs only about $12, for instance; a set of artificial porcelain teeth is $5.95 for a tiger and $1.95 for a coyote, because these are higher quality.

He could buy rubber noses by the gross as well, but usually he moulds the animal's nose out of putty, attaching it to the snout that he shaped from wood or from plaster of Paris and painting it black. Each ear is a piece of soft lead bent so that the skin slips onto it alertly. The eyes are glass; and he has a watchmaker's cabinet of compartments and drawers filled with fox eyes, owl eyes, loon eyes, lynx eyes, coon eyes, lion eyes, snake eyes. Some are veined or show lifelike white corners and carefully differentiate iris and pupil. The catalogue lists twenty-eight sizes, from a buffalo's down to a hummingbird's, and there are cheapjack economy grades, eight pairs for a dollar. He can buy rubber tongues, set into a roll like a wolf's tongue, but unless he is rushed he carves his from wood. He glues the tongue inside the skull, and the lips, gums and roof of the mouth he forms out of wax and then paints them the correct color. Next, he sews and pins the eyelids and cheeks into an appropriate expression and whittles a frame for the neck. He likes to whittle—that basic craft—first using a drawknife, later a delicate spoke-shaver, such as wagon wheels used to be carved with. When only wadding is needed, as for stuffing squirrels and birds, excelsior serves very well, or cotton batting. A bad craftsman would insert the filler as if he were stuffing a cushion, but it's best to wind it tightly first into a credible stance and tie it with thread for permanence. He polishes and lacquers the hooves of the deer and blows with a bellows at the game birds to clean their feathers. Songbirds are wired into a pert pose, wings outspread or beak pointed left; wires bore down through their legs to the varnished perch.

Many droll requests come from customers, surpassing the sort of ideas an undertaker encounters. Some people want blinking lights installed in the eyeholes of the lynx that they've shot. Or they'll put their house thermometer in a deer's leg; they'll want a fat mother porcupine stuffed conventionally but with the fetuses found inside her embalmed in a talcum powder bottle like little rolled-up human babies. A local minister who had served as a missionary in Africa brought back the ears and a foot of an elephant he had shot, and a souvenir strip of leg skin like hard bark. Sometimes a hotel man will buy

167

a pair of bear cubs a farmer has killed and, under the general umbrella of humor, ask that they be preserved in a standing position on their hind legs to hold the ash trays in the lobby. ("Oh, pardon me, little sir, may I use you?")

Understand that I'm making a figurative investigation —the animals native to Vermont which have survived so far are not in danger of quick extinction. The end of subsistence farming has worked to their advantage, and, paradoxically, before the farmers appeared and cleared the land, the Indians of nearby Canada had called this section of New England The Desert because the un-felled timber grew so thick that game was scarce. Still, these modest creatures—flittering does fleeing with a peahen's squawking cry, a pony's hoofbeats, and a car-ousel motion; porcine black bear rooting for mushrooms, rooting for grubs; and all the parade of back-field inhabi-tants, like the varying hares which explode through the ferns and the fire cherry and in winter turn white and nibble ironwood nuts—represent the much bigger ghosts of creatures gone.

Taxidermy, or the notion of saving the scalp, horns and teeth of game, goes along with a fairly advanced stage of settlement. The frontiersmen and homesteaders hunted for meat—it was labor to them, it was feeding the fam-ily; other than furs to dress themselves in, they didn't often keep tokens. The Indians, having evolved a game-oriented religion and culture, were more likely to save an especially superb big skull, but they also killed for use and didn't go in for tricking the animal up as a mannequin. The practice of mounting heads to hang on the wall developed only as the white towns became county seats, long after the first artisans like blacksmiths and carpenters had arrived, when hunters became "sportsmen." Earlier, a fellow might throw a phenomenal skin embodying the memories of real risk and adventure up on the cabin roof to freeze and dry; he might even salt it. By and by the sun would convert the flesh side to a brown board, and it would be tacked in the entryway —that was the taxidermy.

Once in the old gold town of Barkerville, British Columbia, I was talking to a prospector and his wife, both over seventy-five. Their serenity and good cheer were plain; wilderness gardening had obviously agreed with them, so had the solitude, and there was no counting the tonnage of creek sand that they must have panned in a lifetime. But what brought the sense of their achievement home to me as they talked was suddenly to notice two antediluvian grizzly hides hanging in the hallway just behind them: from floor to ceiling, a plush chestnut-brown with darker shades. A basketball player could have enveloped himself in either one with room to spare. Apparently both husband and wife had shot other bears, but had happened to save these. They didn't mention them until I did, and as with every other keepsake they had, didn't stress or boast about the circumstances, just said that the bears had strayed within range on their creek in different years and had seemed to be taking up a settled abode. On a whole host of topics that we touched on, the skins completed what was unsaid.

I'm not against keeping trophies if they define or some-how enlarge the possessor, if they're taken seriously, and if they memorialize the animal world, besieged and war-ranted for an early death as it surely is. Old dirt farm-ers and mild-mannered old taxidermists are outdated too; they will go the way of the wildlife soon. (There is another taxidermist in town, a retired fellow with pouchy cheeks, an upright posture and a face like a squirrel, who keeps his first-prize ribbons from the state fairs of 1911 and 1913 under glass.) This business of my friend's employs three generations. All day outdoorsmen, wearing red shirts or hip boots, drop in and talk, and he and his son and the young boy, scraping the flesh from a black wolf's legs, listen in. They throw sawdust on the floor and handle the beasts that arrive as farmers do their own butchered stock—it lives to live but it lives to be shot. The older man has hunted moose in northern Quebec that put all these little buck deer in the shade, so he's got photographs of the vanished big stuff. When he talks it's always of hunting and game: knolls and ledges to scale, ravines to bypass, and openings which open up as you reach them. Game is like vastly enlivened farm stock; you study it, wish it well, go for the prize.

Along the walls there are shelves of skulls, tagged for insertion into the bear skulls which are being prepared. When the skins are tanned, repairs are made—holes sewn up, bald spots touched over with paint or patched with scraps from another skin. The claws are cleaned, the blemishes concealed, and the obligatory pained-looking snarl, which the animal seldom wore while it was alive, is inscribed on the face. Bear rugs cost the clientele $25 per square foot nowadays, and in a year the shop gets up to seventy of them to work on, though last fall was an unlucky one for hunters because the mast crop was sparse and scattered and a heavy, early snowfall put all the bears in Vermont to bed ahead of time (an estimated thirty-five hundred live in the state). Also, by late November upwards of two hundred deer have been brought in, the floor is heaped high with salted skins, antlers are lying all over the place. Some people want the deer's feet mounted on a plaque under the head and set with an upward poke, to be utilized as a gun rack. The workroom has samples of this arrangement nailed to the walls, and big moose feet, and a great moose head is exhibited, with its pendulous bell, long-suffering ears, and primeval superstructure, bony, leaf-shaped. There's a lovely gray bobcat hanging head down, and a stuffed horned owl, a goshawk, some quail, some black ducks, a Canada goose, a pouter pigeon, two mink, a fox skin, beaver kits, the unfinished head of a coyote with its lips and eyes intricately pinned, and a yearling bear posed standing up, holding a pair of field glasses, as if to help it see better next time.

Snapshots of big men and downed bear, of deer sprawled on the ground and hunters squatting, are tacked on the wall. About fifteen thousand deer a year are killed in Vermont, almost two per square mile, although only one hunter in ten who buys a license is successful in making a kill. The out-of-state hunters do a little bit better statistically, strangely enough, maybe they're at it full time while they're here. Then during the winter perhaps just as many deer starve to death. The deer that we see in the north are still healthy-looking, though there are very few predators left who can prune the herds in a natural fashion, taking the weaker individuals so that the wintering areas are not overgrazed. Bobcats have become scarce because they are hunted year-round, and bobcats aren't really up to the task anyway. Eventually our deer are expected to shrink to the wizened proportions of some of their cousins in southern Vermont or southerly New England, where often the bucks can't even muster the strength to sprout antlers and the fawns that they father are comparably frail—most being shot within the first two or three years of life, in any case. What with the game diminishing in grandeur, the short hunting seasons and complicated regulations, a talented, old-fashioned hunter finds his style crimped. For want of any other game, he exercises himself by hunting coons or the few small surviving predators. One fellow in town, who runs the schoolbuses, a lanky, devoted, preeminent hunter who probably was born too late, goes after bobcats with dogs every weekend all winter, patrolling the snowy deer yards, believing that he is protecting the deer. Bobcats have diminutive chests; they can dash in a burst of speed but soon must get into a tree if the hounds are close, not being equipped for a distance race. A photo shows him with seventeen of the creatures hammered frozen to the side of his house, each with clenched paws and a grimace. He collected the $10 bounty on

172

each, cut off the bobbed tails, and threw the bodies on the town dump.

There is a furred compendium on the tables, a dukedom in furs, not only raccoons and otter and bucks, but skins from the West—grizzly and cougar—as if the supply would never run out. All around the top of the room are fastened dozens of black and white tails—these the whitetail deer tails which they flip up to warn one another when they have cause to bolt, and which they wag vigorously in the fly season, just as a horse does. Almost every evening I watch deer in my field, their coats as red as a red fox. They snort with the sharp sound of a box dropped. Sometimes you only see their tall ears, in a V, the late sunlight shining through pinkly. Originally, a hundred or more years ago, only a moose trail and horse trail wound past where I live. It is exceptionally moosey country, with ponds, mountains, lakes and bogs —country that cries out for moose, in fact. Moose love water. When hard-pressed by wolves, they will spend the whole winter knee-deep in a pond, standing close to where a spring comes in and the water won't freeze; and in the summer, browsing on the bottom, they wade out so far in search of water plants that they finally get in over their heads and push up the tips of their noses every few minutes. The huge bulls, however, are a sight surpassing the vision one had of them, surpassing the mind's inventions. You would think that when they caught sight of themselves reflected on the surface of a smooth lake they would be frightened.

173

Even the bank in town has the head of a moose fixed to the wall, as a remembrance of the old days. It looks like the head of a horse or a cow poking through the half-door of a stable. And looking at it, I get the benign sense of good existing in the world that I have sometimes when I look at a cow—those big ears thrust forward, and those big eyes, as if we all have at least two ways of communicating with each other in this world: sound and sight. A youngster came into the bank while I was there and stared for a long time at the moose head. After a while he went to the door and tried to go through to the other side so that he could see the rest of the animal. To begin with, they had to tell him it wasn't alive.

AMERICANA, ETC.

In 1969 we were engaged in experimenting with ourselves in groups, in getting along in groups, particularly the younger people, who are the ones who need to face the future with more than curiosity. Thus the vast Woodstock Festival and the peace March on Washington, as well as the group-grope contingents who hugged and parried in Encounters. It was a year for seeing whether we really could live civilly in the crowds that the world is coming to or whether the experimenters are right and, like penned rats, we will soon begin eating each other. We found that so far, anyway, we could; as with the other new sensations, we could even have fun. The year was also one in which marital infidelity seemed to become an epidemic, if it hadn't been before, and when a generalized bewilderment ran up and down the land in boots. Indeed, a good many people wore boots, and battened down, wincing at the news broadcasts, exhausted by leapfrogging vogues.

175

Most of the vogues were vogues in loneliness. Girls wore lonely-looking, dragging coats and fashions from the Okie era or the Civil War. There was a vogue in vibrators and stimulators, a vogue in pets, a vogue in chain letters and homey weathermen who talked the way the man next door might talk if neighbors in the city talked.

I used to love to get into the thick of crowds. I loved the subway rush hour, the crush at ticket windows, the squeeze of New Year's Eve on Forty-second Street, or the night street market in Boston. I felt enlarged, recharged by these mob scenes, much as I did when climbing on a mountainside. The tussling beefiness of everybody poured into me like broth; I felt exuberant, enhanced by the soul-mix. I liked losing control of where my feet took me, I liked swimming against the tide and with the tide. I liked feeling united with many, many other men, becoming all together as big as Gulliver, sprawled bulkily and uncoordinatedly along the street. And though I'd seen mobs behave savagely, some of my experience was of the moments when, on the contrary, a benign expressiveness, even a kind of *sweetness,* is loosed—when life seems to be an unmixed good, the more the merrier, and each man rises to a sense of glee and mitigation, alleviation or freedom which perhaps he wouldn't quite dare feel alone. The smiling lightness, infectious blitheness, the loose exultant sense of unity in which sometimes a mass of people as a whole seem to improve upon the better nature of the parts—this intrigued me. Figuratively it manifests itself for instance in the extraordinary quality that singing by a congregation acquires. The humdrum and unlovely voices gradually merge into a sweet, uniquely pristine note, a note angelic-sounding, hardly believable. Looking about, one can't see who in particular might have such a voice; everybody in the pew wears an expression as if he were about to sneeze, and squawks at least a little. It is a note created only when hundreds sing. It needs them all; no single person is responsible, any more than any individual in a roaring mob lends that its bestiality.

Just as with other natural wonders of the world to which one relinquishes oneself, instead of feeling smaller, I often felt bigger when I was packed into a multitude, and taking for granted the potential for mayhem of crowds, of which so much has been written, I was fascinated instead by the clear pealing gaiety, the swelling savory relief and regenerative power that sometimes overrides the anxieties we suffer from when we're alone and lets us stand there beaming on the pavement with twenty thousand other people. It's like riding in surf, it's like a Dantean ascent one circle up. Suddenly we *like* all of these strangers—even the stranger in ourselves—and seem to see a shape to life, as if all the exertions of the week really were justified and were a source of joy.

On the other hand, my daydreams at this stage usually involved triumphs of solitude, like Lawrence riding in Arabia, because great open barren spreading space was necessary for any true victory. Since such space had already ceased to exist, I settled for the idea that moving around a lot was freedom enough: a bleak and friendless start in a new place would furnish the leeway of

space. The reaction is a common one, and so we have
our job shifts and change-of-address routines, moving
from Delaware to Phoenix. Young men move and move
and move again, enjoying their invisibility, enjoying being lonely (crowds in this case are a desert). Circus and
carnival life attracted me especially and much of the al-
lure was on this same basis—to be anonymous, a traveler
through thickets of cities, to be nearly as alone as if in
Arabia and yet surrounded by huge crowds daily. It was
winy to me. I dipped into the two sensations: the solitude (while I was working in the circus, quite literally
I took care of the camels), and yet the comradeship of
immense crowds, renewed in every town, crowds which
began forming at 4 A.M.—maybe two or three thousand
people right at the railroad yards as we pulled in.

The circus provided universal entertainment for anyone with eyes to see. First the procession to the lot, with
elephants and painted wagons and caravans of flighty
horses; the tents were slowly lifted; the cookhouse stove-
pipes started smoking. The Midway was public property,
and then with the band music drifting through the side-
walls, a crowd sometimes almost as large as that inside
the Big Top stood around the rope barriers of the "backyard" during the hubbub of the night performance. Before each spectacle, custardy ruffled frosted floats bearing
lighted castles and ballet girls perched in them were
hauled into position. The tumblers practiced flips, their
voices as tense as barks as they prepared themselves, and
horse-holders and spear-carriers ran around hitching the
teams, adjusting the gaudy-looking carpets on the floats,

grinning at the girls and giving latecomers a foot up. The elephants arrived, with their imperial howdahs on, galumphing, as ponderous as Hannibal's army but carrying the accumulated grace of twenty centuries. They took hoops in their mouths and more girls sat and swung in these, rocking gently as the beasts walked. The clowns got into line, and the jugglers, the costume mistress dressed as the Queen of Hearts, trained palominos drumming their feet, and several strange stalking ladies who released pigeons on signal. There was the racket of the tractors working, of generator engines; shrill whistles blew; and in the meantime the canvasmen, the cookhouse crew, menagerie men, prop handlers and ringstock roustabouts gathered around, wiping the crumbs from supper off their mouths and squinting at the leggy girls as into a spotlight. The splendor and the smells, the wealth and deprivation, the jammed exotic mass islanded in flooding lights, fairytale figures leaping to life in plaster masks and sequined frocks (Jack Horner, Goldilocks), and fleshly glamor girls, and pachyderms like African kings in thick brocade, swaying and heralding themselves with French-horn honks and waving trunks—we ragged Bedouin types darting in and out were the connective tissue of all this. Inspired as the circus was, we were its gristle and we made it so.

I'd stand as part of that—larger than myself, larger than life—and then I'd go to the Midway and mingle with the hordes of people there: the children and the hawkers and the gazing grownups who were shoulder to shoulder and pink and ivory in the lights. It was children's night, lovers' night, a night for taking things at face value, a night for smiling and for spending freely. Finally when the grounds had emptied and the performers had gone downtown to their hotels, if we were staying another day, people in my position looked for a pile of straw to make a bed on, under the stars Bedouin style, or underneath the lions' cage if rain was falling. Of course I loved the lions' roaring—it sauced my dreams— the restless feet over my head. I dreamt adventurously, and because robberies often occurred after midnight among the gang of roughies sleeping along the ground, to lie under the lions' cage was safer than most places; their stringent smell, their paws that eloquently hung out between the bars scared off the thieves.

Gloom and fastidiousness have diluted these pleasures for me. The lions which are left have enough to do just being seen. It would probably be necessary to organize an unbroken line of spectators five abreast shuffling past their cages in every zoo around the world in order to give everybody alive a glimpse of one, and private experiences with them, such as I had, are not so easily obtainable. I wouldn't like to live as a Bedouin now; I haven't got the stomach for it; and I don't go looking for crowds either—I extricate myself from random crushes on the street before I'm pinned, being quite an expert at foreseeing how they will develop, as a former aficionado. Occasionally I do still steep myself in the few great incidents of herding that arise, however, because even now there is more meaning in the unexpected exhilaration of being a mote in a vast winding creature buoyed by itself, rolling across a rolling mall, than one can account for. The sudden simplicity of joy is still puzzling, and if we are seldom able to settle on what we think of ourselves, at least we see the way we sometimes lift our heads and catch the beat of other people's good intentions, queue up with them for the sake of their company, and beam and grin as if we're glad to have been born—as if we even find it reasonable. Though most of us no longer feel inklings of an existence after life, we do somehow have to take into consideration this big mystifying infusion of euphoria which comes to us in crowds.

A crowd oscillates around its edges like a swimming skate, and by moving forward it's possible to experience the tight squeeze of Dunkirk or the hysteric press of the real claustrophobes who struggle at the center: then by backing away, the easy chummy nudging of people who do not know each other but seem to be in optimistic agreement anyway, who catch each other's yawns and jokes. The best crowds are made up of city people, who are used to close conditions, wise at the tactics and the etiquette. It's among them you see the sidelong, tacit, essential politeness, when the event is good-humored— a sense of space as being commonly owned. There is a silent, round-and-round and to-and-fro motion occurring in crowds, a sort of mesmeric Brownian motion which makes a sane participation possible. Each person strolls as though the space at hand were limitless, keeping counsel with himself, though constantly altering course in order to avoid collisions. It's like deficit high finance, where more money is used than actually exists because what does exist is out on loan in several directions. Turning, tacking to and fro, everybody borrows and reborrows space as from a common hoard. If they are enormous and purposeful and yet peaceable enough, such scenes give us a kick like the earth's other great natural sights—waterfalls, high wooded bluffs. We gulp them in, believe in them, without knowing exactly what it is that we're believing.

I wasn't at Woodstock or on the beach at Cape Canaveral for the Moonshot; my only crowd fest for the summer was the Orleans County Fair in north Vermont. But this was a hunk of the same phenomenon—exhilarating and exhausting, and somewhat of a mystery. Upwards of twenty thousand people attended; it's one of the large fairs, over a century old as a fete and an occasion, and I got headaches from going to it continually; squinting with relief, I watched the last trucks leave when the week ended. Nothing culturally explosive had happened, nothing that wouldn't have happened before the Second World War, for example, but I'd gazed on Americana by the acre, and steeped myself in the biscuity smell of people packed together, pacing through the dust, celebrating the short north-country summer.

Like other county fairs, the Orleans Fair serves to measure the energy of the local business groups who organize it and reassures everybody, even the summer visitors, that this neck of the woods is not just a watered-down vacation package but has a concreteness its own.

Although the fairs do need some subsidizing now—the Orleans promoters get about $10,000 from Vermont's racetrack take—this only compensates them for the competition which more modern diversions provide. As in earlier days, circus acts, hell drivers and comedians must be hired; there are trotting races, raffles, craft and livestock competitions; and a carnival is on hand. So many events take place that nobody can see them all. The Fair Association's thirty-five directors are citizens whose own work usually relates to one of the specialties on the program. Farmers supervise the cattle judging; there are horsemen for the horse show, loggers to oversee the ox pulling, and a machinery dealer helps out with the tractor rodeo. The ticket manager is an insurance agent, and the State's Harness Racing Commissioner, who lives close by, arranges the racing program and books the grandstand show.

The president of the fair is a controversial, indefatigable auto dealer named Howard Conley, who has pushed operations out of the red the past few years. In July, at the dedication of the new Floral Hall, a kind of backlash love-in was held for him, with Vermont's governor speaking, because *Life* magazine had written up Conley as the father of a young man who shot into a Negro newcomer's house one night, vigilante-fashion, and then nearly got off scot-free. The state police are estimated to have lavished 2,256 man-hours on the case, mostly investigating the Negro. Conley is a fidgety, thin, Appalachian type, bony and acquisitive, and yet sometimes impulsively generous —loyal, down-homey, hard-driving and shrewd. He limps, and looks personable enough, not like a civil-rights villain, unless perhaps when he laughs, and has a handsome, strapping wife. The several Confederate bumper stickers around town, certain writing on the walls of the telephone booths, and the defensive, unhappy air in his office when I went there to leave a note, indicated that the township has divided into camps for and against him, but it was hard to find anybody who would admit they were against. The publicity about the episode seemed to have hurt and amazed him, nevertheless, and made him hesitant and shy. His pride in the fair as it got going, the vim he threw into the jobs at hand, seemed an attempt at vindication, and he was rather touching at times.

Three days before Opening Day the miscellaneous collection of vehicles comprising *Smoky Gilmore's Greater Shows* began to arrive. Humpy, shabby trucks, long trailer rigs loaded with numbered dismantled equipment, and camper pickups and snug house trailers with blinds in the windows and Southern license plates pulled onto the lot. Parking in convoys until Smoky got around to assigning space, the drivers dozed. Smoky, whose home base is Strong, Maine, is a lumbering, somnolent-bodied fat man with a wolf's bright eyes. He cast these over the stretch of ground available to him and paced off a few distances, calculating where he'd fit the rides and games, while munching a cheese sandwich from the food stand which the Irasburg Grange was setting up. Meanwhile his carny roustabouts in cowboy hats with Aussie brims circled the lot with an Alsatian dog which had a glass eye, surveying where they would be living for the next week. The various Grange ladies were sprucing up the grounds, and the watchmen and handymen were shoveling mud out of the entrances to the grandstand. A bulldozer worked on the road in front of the barns, filling in potholes; some boys were tossing straw into the stalls. The carnival and grandstand faced the row of barns across the half-mile track. Inside the track was the announcer's tower, the stage platform, and a thriving expanse of grass where the thousands of cars would park.

For me, the fair offered a chance to taste again the delectations of my life of nearly twenty years ago—the uproar and the heat, the loneliness of slipping through a mob, the atmosphere of smothered violence—and yet go home to wife and child and mountain farmhouse in the dusk, leaving the hullabaloo behind. The circus hasn't fared well since when I knew it. Several unions began to menace it with organizing drives, the railroads which transported it started to founder, the public lost the fresh wide-eyed delight needed for itinerant extravaganzas. Temporary personnel could not be recruited so easily and the way of life came to seem punishing and grueling, even unnatural, to the circus types themselves: living mostly out of doors, traveling nearly every night, performing in a new place the next day with the wind currents jostling them. The pay was bad, the dedication required of a performer was almost monastic, so they preferred at least the comfort of week-long engagements indoors under the auspices of organizations like the Shriners, who guaranteed expenses. But once the tents were put away, more and more circuses folded, and often acts were booked

185

individually for the arena shows. By contrast, a carnival is harder to dismember or to move indoors or subject to efficiency procedures, and carnival "jumps" are leisurely and infrequent compared to the continual peregrinations of a circus. The overhead is low; the show operates twelve hours a day; and the few jobs on the lot need no lifelong outlay of discipline or expertise on the part of anyone.

Usually a carnival is a collection of independent concessionaires who gather each year under the aegis of one energetic man who may own only a few of the rides himself but who does the negotiating for all the rest for a percentage of their take. Smoky was paying the Fair Association about $11,000 for the privilege of setting up shop during Fair Week, and Conley's group then distributed much of this money among the novelty and thrill performers who had been hired to do two shows a day in front of the grandstand. The carnival depended upon the fair to draw good crowds, in other words, and paid for the service, but the fair itself depended on the circus-style daredevil or variety acts to bring the crowds to the fairgrounds in the first place. The fair charged an admission at the gate and with this other source of income paid for the prizes, raffles and what not, breaking even when the State's subsidy came in, as well.

Smoky's show is fairly free of gyp devices, and I noticed that most of the hardies operating the rides were boys who were adventuring, or sturdy knock-about hoboes, not the lunatics and dazed fellows just out of jail and bitter-mouthed bad-luck-histories who work in many carnivals. A circus feeds its personnel, but a carnival is laissez-faire; every man eats whatever he can get his hands on. Staying longer in each little town, he and his cronies aren't as set apart and self-sufficient as circus men, churning along under their own power; they're linked to New England or the U.S. instead of to a self-contained, tradition-bound and death-defying fraternity which is rooted in Europe. A circus has a special whirlwind momentum and glory, the craft of a lifetime piled on the craft of previous lifetimes, whereas a carnival does not give performances but provides games and equipment on which the townsfolk may amuse themselves. The carny boys sit on stools beside the tractor engines that drive the machinery, shifting gears and watching for the wallets that are dropped or that fly off centrifugally. In the old days sometimes these boys did so poorly that they would let themselves be locked into the vendors' wagons to sleep when it was raining. The vendors didn't trust them but they would do them that much of a favor, and if it was slightly creepy to be behind padlocks, at least the boys were dry. Now they can afford to bunk downtown in a hotel and feast on London broil, instead of wolfing leftover pretzels and cream soda. And yet the tales survive of raffish, snake-oil carnies traveling through small towns and playing the hicks for fools. Most of us like to think of the carnies as triumphing—we take the viewpoint of Mark Twain—but up here in Vermont the contest wasn't seen from that angle. As the fair's opening approached, the stories told were just the opposite: of farm hands getting their money back, of young kids ganging up on the carnie man in righteous wrath and pulling his tent down.

The girlie shows appeared: Puss 'n Boots, The Dancing Dollies, The French Quarter, and Casa Kahlua. Each of the four consisted of a truck, a tent, two ladies in residence, and two or three hard-guy young touts to ride shotgun for them.

Guy Gossing drove overnight from Providence with eight tigers in a moving van. He had a broken hand, a hopping limp, forearms stitched with scars, a thousand lines in his forehead, a down-drawn mouth with windswept elements of humor behind it, and triangular, fatalistic blue eyes. He was short, blond and burned and looked like an old Africa hand, which indeed he was, although originally from Belgium. Driving the van was obviously not his idea of fun—he hardly spoke enough English to ask directions if he had to. He was dismayed and depressed upon arriving and sat in a camp chair in a feminine artistic grump because no chute or proper facilities for his act cage to stand on had been built. His wife was cooking a Continental-smelling lunch, however, and Conley came over, agreeably chatty and cosmopolitan for the moment, not rawhide-hillbilly, and set the carpenters to work.

The Cyclonians, Charlie Van Buskirk and wife, also showed up, Buskirk with a sprained ankle sustained at his last gig down in Pennsylvania. He looked more like an emperor's footman than a unicyclist, being statuesque, with waxed mustaches, and yet as shuffling and happy-go-lucky onstage as a college dropout, but he said that his father had had a troupe of unicyclists and had trained him from babyhood. His wife was a former adagio dancer, so their act blended both trades. A pleasant fellow, Buskirk has a rundown farm outside Rochester that he gets to about one month a year, and says he likes the alternation of performing outdoors in the summer and indoors in the winter.

Other performers rolled in, driving from different points: the Manuel Del Morals, two tumbler brothers who look like the President of Mexico photographed twice, and the Gutis, small German strong men with wizened skin, almost dwarflike, who play gorillas in costume and enact a bullfight. They're impersonal and polished, longtime veterans of circus life. The Sensational Leighs, acrobats, had hurried through bad weather from Milwaukee (he with a temperature of 102, stopping along the way for shots), where they had seen a big top blow down next to them in a windstorm. Nodding to the rest—most of them had met before—they pulled their trailer into the covered-wagon protective square where everybody parked behind the stage. The agent who had booked the groups was on hand too, a tiny, clever, barber-like man who sat reading *Billboard* when there weren't any little flare-ups of temperament to be smoothed over—he'd rise and walk quickly to Floral Hall, telling jokes softly but rapid-fire, and then withdraw, refusing me an interview, much like a boxer's cornerman.

To be successful a country fair needs a rural county to draw on for its events and spirit—yet not a county that is so rural it is empty. By Wednesday, when the gates officially opened, the crowds were on the scene and growing. Lithe slender trotters exercised on the racetrack, going by like gala ribbons, shining with well-bred sweat. The cattle judging was under way, a slow, quiet proceeding with few spectators but a great many animals, who were being looked at by three men hired from outside the state. A slim cowboy in boots judged the beef breeds only, the Anguses and Herefords, and spoke into the microphone diffidently to explain each decision ("clean in the neck, strength of loins"). The Anguses were muscly, black and squat like boars, with a low center of gravity and square wide ears; the Herefords looked like orangutans, their legs a bit longer, their bodies blotted with orange and postured as solidly as a large ape's. The Holsteins and Guernseys—big pro milkers that feed America's schoolchildren—were judged by a tense lyric man with a kind heart, who practically sang his summations. "She won by her spread of rump, depth of body, and that terrific set of legs, her whole top-line, and her dairy promise, the shapeliness of the udder and teat placement, the mammary system—she's just so very *dairy* with that udder promise!"

Calves, yearlings, two-year-olds, mature animals, fat hornless bulls with testicles like udders, and assorted combinations, the get of one sire or one dam, were displayed. Watching the gradual fleshing out of the heifers, the fickle distribution of natural gifts, and then the aging, it became like watching the march from birth to death of all creatures, as the contests, successively involving older and older classes, went on late into the afternoon and the next day. The Jerseys appeared overshadowed by the bigger specialized dairy breeds, but they were as dainty as does and the same pretty color, and they interested me because they were the cows of my boyhood. They and the Ayrshires were judged by a Canadian cattle breeder, a natty white-haired man with a sharp Scottish nose, level-eyed and dry in mood, who wore a sport coat and a crew cut. He tilted his fedora against the sun, and as he studied the animals, signaled the owners with brief, somber gestures to turn them or to line them up in orderly fashion for a march-past, not speaking till the end. He gave his verdict in a low, easy voice. "I'm placing number one over number two because of her balance and walk, her flesh, which is neater up front, laid in more neatly in the shoulder and the rib, her glands, and the attachment of her teats." Between shows he drives all night—from here he was going to Three Rivers, Quebec. Watching him straightening a cow's tail to see its set, sometimes twitting the farmer as well with a significant twist of his wrist, it was clear he enjoyed his work. Whole families were present, dressed in white milking suits and wearing glasses, swallowing their smiles, moving their sensitive-looking nostrils. The father would exhibit the cow he considered his best, his wife the second-best, and so on down to their youngest child. But after a rigorous inspection, the Canadian judge might choose the five-year-old girl's cow over the others, to her papa's astonishment, and give the blue ribbon to her.

As at a ball park, you can eat supremely badly if you

want to: cold hot dogs from East St. Louis and dirty buns. Instead, I went to the Eureka Grange to have sweet corn and warm blueberry muffins. The girlie shows lay low during the afternoon, but the carnival rides whirled round and round. A pinto pony, furry, chipper and haughty, with a mane so thick in front of its eyes that it could hardly see, was raffled off. A boy with high-set cheeks won and for the rest of the fair rode around the grounds, seated straight up like a trooper; he was the winner that the pony needed. I went to Floral Hall to check the vegetables: limpid translucent onions and shiny green peppers, speckly cauliflowers, bagged brown potatoes, fat green tomatoes, along with understated boxes of eggs. There were lovely summer vegetables like beets, chicory and butternut squashes tagged with prize ribbons and heaped together in a kitchen pan as if for supper, and chocolate cakes, canned venison, and maple candy, and soap cakes carved, and afghans, woolen mittens, and rugs woven from baling twine. Also, inevitably, the utility company was pulling its oar with an exhibit; a service club had a tableau advocating motherhood; and among the motor vehicles in the commercial section I was brought up short by a tombstone display.

At the grandstand Don D., the emcee, an indoor-looking man in a cowpoke suit, was trying to lead the crowd in "The Marine's Hymn," with maybe less response than he'd expected—his notions about Vermont were hawkish. Happy Dave, the clown, performing first as Happy Davis, made up in sad-face, talked to his hat, miming explana-

192

tory squibs, and had some trouble with his trampoline—
said a mock prayer. He tugged off a series of vests and,
finally, a bra, and got two legs in one leg of his baggy
dungarees before at last stripping down to a striped gym
suit and doing somersaults high in the air while puffing a
cigar. Later on, without the bulbous nose, he appeared
as Dave Hanson, driving a "1913 Rolls Rotten" which
spurted firecrackers, seemed to catch fire, and ultimately
threw him in one grand explosion right through the roof.
He wore a flat hat and overalls with ruby writing on them
and was awfully weary of that carful of slapstick stuff
when he came off the track. He's the tough clown, banging through his routines, pepper-talking like a movie
newspaperman, machinegunning his words; he is a law-
and-order buff, a bitter guy, an honorary member of the
Pottstown, Pa., police force, with a strong yen to join full
time. He talks of car smashups, and the effect a shotgun
blast has on its victim. When you look closely, even his
makeup breaks down to rat-tat points under the eyes.

The booking agent reminisced about when Ginger
Rogers broke into show business. He himself got started
with an act in which, using his fingers, he projected
shadow figures on the wall. The clown was talking about
the flattening impact of .45-caliber gunfire. The emcee
left the stage after bullying the audience with his latest
singalong ("The Battle Hymn of the Republic"), making
them clap two or three times. He is a sallow lady-killer
with pockets underneath his eyes. The strange thing about
him is his incongruous voice, all mellifluence and volume.

When the clown kidded him about the quality of his humor, he said he wasn't going to expend his best stuff on a crowd like this one.

Guy Gossing had driven to the slaughterhouse in Lyndonville for beef hearts for his cats. Now it was night. The shadows were even more fancifully vivid than the lights—long glamorous amber shadows. The tigers, smelling like ouzo-and-straw, lay on their backs, propping their legs against the bars, their paunches showing, and Gossing woke them up before the act to start them scrapping and roaring. "Allah! Rajah! Bengal!" Mrs. Gossing, a Chinese-faced Belgian housewife, shrieked the names, too, to remind them that they were outnumbered. They roared like motorcycles and lunged and slunk, a fine youthful passel of tigers. It's a good fighting act when Gossing chooses to exert himself. He's a journeyman trainer, a fellow tired of it now but who knows all the jumps and moves, whether or not he ever was able to do the stoutest feats himself. Like any aging professional tired of his work and touring the hinterlands, he's ready to be lackluster if there is no occasion to be more than that, but by hopping quickly to stay off his bad leg, chasing and punching the cats, escalating each spark of resistance on their part, milking every chance for furor, hefting the heavy stools and pretending to fight his way along the bars, he can recapture his old flair. Still, there's a lot of wasted rigamarole with them on their stools, sitting up, or posing in a row on their hind legs leaning against a horizontal pole. He forces one up on top of a ball and has her foot it along a metal track; then has the eight of them roll over and over on the ground in pairs, to wind up lined up close, alert and gorgeous in an orange mass, with all heads turned toward him. It isn't really very much, and to add action and enthusiasm, he makes the tigers move around, and jogs, and shifts the furniture, and whips the air, evincing modest ferocity. His wife, sluggish but shrill—she's the eyes in back of his head—yells any tiger's name who seems to be stirring. Gossing, wearing a short-sleeved shirt, looks like a sunburned Congo mercenary, and unless you have no sympathy for aging athletes, you cheer him on.

Billiard balls seem to enjoy themselves. Painted brightly, they seem to revel in the zigzag sociability of the table, crowding each other, then flying apart. Birds flock in, flock out like flying sparks, and water spiders run away and run together in ticktocking compatibility, and the Brownian motion of crowds is similar. All of us meandered at the fair, averting collisions as carelessly as if it were part of the mechanism by which we walked. We strolled with many turns and stops, paying little attention to our neighbors but with no object in mind so fixed that it couldn't be abandoned if the path was blocked. Our whimsy was our freedom.

The carnival, operating with almost equal intricacy, had the same aura about it of participation in a grand design. The Octopus—six angular arms with buckets on the ends—reeled in a circle round and round, each bucket revolving on its own axis. The Round-up, a centripetal device, started flat, like a potter's wheel, and then stood up on edge, with the riders pressed hard against the rim. The Scrambler was a thicket of buckets mixing and jibing at great speed. There were Bumper-cars; a carousel with a small but effective organ—tin-tin, tub-tub —and bleached but convulsive horses; a Tilt-a-whirl, which was a rattling dizzy ride supervised by a broken-nosed movie star from Texas; and my favorite, the Tip Top, a Humpty-Dumpty-like creation which bounced on cushions and blasts of air while playing goofy wheezy nursery music as it turned. The mechanical activity—big Allis-Chalmers engines pistoning under a subtler, wider roil—gave the carnival some of the sweeping majesty of a steamship which makes shuttle crossings and doesn't regis-ter its significance by where it's going so much as by what's going on within its hub of lights. The roaring rides, the string of pitch games and shooting galleries with feathery prizes, the local Legionnaires offering their ver-sions of craps and roulette, all amounted to a vast river-boat that was traveling slowly through town. Sometimes the machines ran the men and sometimes the men en-joyed their dominion over the machines, but though the announcer for the hell drivers apologized to the crowd many times for the fact that they weren't astronauts and seemed dejected on account of the Moonshot, nobody who worked in the carnival felt in the least eclipsed by this event.

Freak shows are a vanishing item of Americana, how-ever. The Phineas T. Barnum "gallery of weirdos" was "sculpturistic and pictorial," according to the spiel, mean-ing that the spectator would have to make do with plaster

196

models and photographs. You could see "Miss Betty Lou Williams, born to go through life with her baby sister growing out of her stomach, and Zip the Pinhead, Glommo the Human Garbage Can, Grace McDaniels the Mule-faced Girl, too ugly to go to school, and Little Frieda Pushnik, the Living Torso." Freak-show faces are ordinary, homely faces which have been brought to a tragic apotheosis—there may be a usefulness in seeing them, in other words. But freak shows are disappearing from carnivals because the naïveté that gawked at Grace McDaniels is now surfeited with war and medical science and the old commonplace, neighborly appeals to one's half-smirking sense of mercy and of sadism. We who have stayed far away from Vietnam for these past years are nevertheless shellshocked; we are survivors. P. T. Barnum, like Noah Webster, is now in the public domain, so anything may be offered under the cover of his name. These photographs, not wrenched or tragic but simply blurred, represented the one kind of gyp Barnum didn't impose on the public. He gave people a laugh or a lesson, but never *nothing* for their money.

Ox pulling is another fading game. Oxen crossed the country, logged, dragged freight wagons for a century, and plowed the plains, yet you see them at only a few fairs. Judging from the Orleans contests, ox pulling is in its final amateurish throes as a sporting event and might be better accepted as dead. It *is* a start to see those ornamental antique-looking ox yokes actually worn instead of fastened over somebody's door; it's like seeing a bald eagle close up. The animals are docile, bland, smooth-skinned; they seldom seem to act, only react. Except for their color they look like water buffaloes, and have big horns and empty dangling scrotums. Blocks of cement, each weighing a thousand pounds, are lifted by fork-lift onto a sort of metal toboggan, called the boat, which the competing teams drag as far as they can. A measurement is recorded and then a tractor with a winch pulls the boat back again. But the men were rusty at handling the oxen and the oxen seemed to have been hastily trained, as though as a weekend hobby; either the drivers were clumsily embarrassed with them or else angrily agitated and cruel. An oxlike old fellow in green overalls with vicious-looking X suspenders and glinting eyeglasses bashed the noses of his team incessantly with the butt of his whip with all his strength regardless of whether or not they pulled with a will. Maneuvering them was so difficult, apparently, that I was glad when the contest was over, glad that tractors had been invented. The brutes, who had been munching grass before the action started, stood bushed and bewildered, twisting in their yokes like collared boys.

That evening, the pony pull was quite a different proposition—brisk, jingly and eventful, like a living Western, and with a partnership between the men and teams. There were many spectators, many young men competing. The dusk, too, lent the scene a romantic flavor, and the ponies' polished harnesses were studded with brass. The ponies responded to the announcer's instructions, taking their places quickly and throwing themselves into the pull. The drivers put their hands on the rumps of the teams and convivially helped them heave. A pony pair weighing a total of 990 pounds pulled 4000 ("forty hundred") pounds of cement for sixteen inches. A team that weighed 1100 pounds pulled the same load twenty-two inches and won. The feat is done with a tremendous jerk applied immediately as the hitch is made, and so, because of the nervousness of the ponies, the moment of making the hitch is like the tension around a starting gate—everybody, the people and the ponies, knowing what is about to happen and anticipating. Whipping is not permitted, whereas the oxen had suffered all the penalties which the world dishes out to the stupid.

On Saturday and Sunday afternoons the full-sized horses pulled—these actual workhorses employed for skidding logs out of the woods. Big Percherons, heavily shod, they were called Dan & Tom, and Duke & Jim, Dick & Spike, Queen & Molly, and other cheerful names like that. The tourney was "Open to the World," meaning to entries from Canada, and it was very busy, with numerous teams waiting, their handlers rubbing them and running around, maybe not as animated or swift a sight as the pony pulling but more intimate and professional and appealing. Again the teams were classed by weight—up to 3000 pounds, 3200 pounds, 3500 pounds, and the free-for-all, which can include any two horses alive. Indeed, the teams can weigh up to two tons, and for a brief inspired instant may pull up to ten tons. Six tons was the most I saw pulled, but I was astonished that such a rockpile could be moved even a foot. "We're trying to keep our kids on the farm, trying to keep them from running to the city," said Payson Davis, the fair's entertainment director, and it seemed that by rights the horse pull ought to help, if anything would. A Dalmatian dashed about, encouraging his master's team; the husky young drivers pitched in, assisting each other, and whooped and smoked and gossiped as twilight fell. I noticed that although the boys in the carnival had wilder hair and cursed a little more often, their faces and those of these loggers and farm hands were not different. The poverty and hard woods life and winter nights beside an iron stove had marked some of the local people similarly.

The oxen and the tigers we had watched were on the path to oblivion—the tigers were striped for extinction just like a doomed building's windows. But this tic-like strolling and seethe of human beings shopping for entertainment—the auto-smash show scheduled hard on the heels of period-piece presentations—were in the current mode.

The hell drivers had driven from Toronto after a late performance to play the Orleans Fair on Sunday, and they slept across the front seats of their crash cars, leaving the doors open for extra space; all morning they were on view, asleep. "Champions, stand by! . . . Signal Six, all champions! . . . Danger takes to the raceway! . . . " Badgering their cars, they drove through flames, did "cross-overs" and hurdled "elevations." Sideburned, rangy young men who looked like unsteady mechanics, they limped along the racetrack in tennis shirts, white pants and boots, and were a masculine equivalent to the girlies, being much admired, much despised.

A girlie is a girl who strips, but where the emphasis formerly was on her procrastinations in going about doing this, now it's a matter of how fast and directly she gets the garments off, since she is racing a hundred girlfriends and bar-and-grill pickups. While she is in the public eye outside the tent, she dances in the old-fashioned filmy robes with bumps and grinds, but when the customers have been segregated inside, away from abstainers and wives and kids, she simply walks through the curtain and proffers her bare body to be licked by those close to the stage for five or ten minutes, until the time is up. Striptease is gone; the girlie is pressing against the barriers of human sacrifice. If someone bites her hard she screams and the exhibition is cut short.

Although Vermont isn't a state where one would go planning to see blue movies, on the other hand, the sort of rural area where night riders can shoot into a house and not be denied community support and the support of the police may not be as conservative in its social customs as it's cracked up to be. The really cunnilingual girlie shows, where "lunch is served"—much stronger spectacles than the skin flicks that city men see—travel between agricultural towns on the back ridges, whether in New England or Tennessee. At the Orleans Fair, the big drawing card with the Catholic Canadians across the border a few miles away was what they could expect to glimpse in these four tents, so having a high attendance at the other programs on the fairgrounds partly depended upon satisfying their expectations. It didn't seem peculiar, in any case: farming people are familiar with nakedness.

201

Two shows were owned by a fellow named Bob, who also managed the other two for an absentee owner. Bob was a New Yorky barker, fast-talking, factual, hard-shelled but fair. He was stocky, in his forties, and enjoyed confiding to the crowd how tough the life was on the girls, a pair of whom were at his side like two leashed mink, dancing in the heat and cold. "Two hard-working girls. They've been working hard all summer and they're going to work hard all fall." Neither was specifically sexy except for the fact they were up there go-going to the Rolling Stones. One had the face of a British shopgirl and one looked like Andy Warhol. They smiled at Bob's jokes glazedly, staring over the upturned heads. As the night darkened and the Midway crowd grew thick and bold, mostly they worked inside, only reappearing to assure the fellows in the ticket line that Casa Kahlua was a live show, and to catch a breath of air and shake the spittle off themselves.

Next door, at Puss 'n Boots, a black-haired boy from Boston rasped into a microphone, "Red-hot ramble, long and strong; they strip to please and not to tease," with a grimace of real distaste, as if he were pulling a cross-cut saw. He had a coed winker beside him, with curly hair down to her shoulders, a heart-shaped face, a sweetheart smile—a tireless flirter, straight from the ivied halls, she said. She was the beauty of the fairgrounds and loved the exposure, the gazing, pushing guys; she picked out individuals to play to outside, ducking through the curtains with coaxing glances to strip for the spendthrifts inside. She had the flushed look of a college girl—stoned, loving

202

the evening, yet about to cry. Matched with her was a lethargic fat blond substitute flown in the day before, who was an experienced stage caryatid but wholly a neophyte at this carny grab bag. She had her little daughter with her and her husband—a Simple Simon type—and was being hurt at nearly every performance because, sulky, joyless, she made only the required moves. "Too many hands! Handle with care!" yelled the big balding ticket-taker, like a bookkeeper gone wrong. "Be nice!" she said, watching everybody apprehensively; but the men, who had been awed by the pretty coed, moved to make up for their restraint with her. "Will you be nice?" she asked each guy. He would promise, but then he'd cup her thighs like a melon and bite.

The Dancing Dollies—a small china doll with compressed face and a trim, giddy short-haired redhead—exercised diligently like majorettes. The redhead seemed sorrowful and abandoned, and looked like girls I knew. The barker was a sailorly beefy native of Maine. "Showtime! Alley oop!" he cried. He had a rug merchant competing with him for lung power (rugs of the Yellowstone and the Last Supper), as well as the traditional hammer-and-bell—three swings for a quarter, and a nickel cigar if you managed to ring the bell. The Green Hornets, motorcyclists, were at it, stirred up by the sight of the girls; the old man who ran the concession bent humbly next to their brawn.

Inside the girl tents, the vulnerable, androgynous bodies were like a shower room: flesh-colored, breadboard backs and dabs of pubic hair. A Southern heavyweight from

Selma spieled for the French Quarter, chuckling his words like dirty jokes until the farmers' smiles changed to pie-eating grins. He had the assistance of a yellow-haired belle called Penny, a hot mama who waddled. In the tent, she caught hold of a codger and polished his pate with her fat boobs and rubbed his glasses on her pussy. "Be nice. Be like you aren't," she told the customers, making them clap like seals. The early birds had been determined middle-class persons, embarrassed to be there, ashamed but curious, standing with their arms crossed, hoping none of their friends would spot them and ripe for bullying. Later, the Johns climbed the tent pole; a roll of chicken wire was laid along the sidewall to prevent sneak-ins, gang rapes and such events. The loggers of French Canada were fighting to get in the entrance and the girls scarcely needed to show themselves outside on the platform, or when they did they simply sat resting with their legs crossed. Like politicians who no longer listen to dinner speeches but who know when to smile, they kept track of when they were supposed to appear robed and when they should be in the nude.

This Penny knew the motions and was unflagging as a man, leaving the people puffing. If she hadn't coached her relief girl, whose name was Susie Wong, they probably would have ripped Susie apart in retaliation. Susie was a dumb-eyes with small mishandled breasts, a hanging plume of hair, an inaudibly piping voice, and was a girl who looked undressed no matter how much she had on because she kept her mouth moistened and open. She had a boyish, sexual, scrawny body, a slim cat face, and somehow represented the entire southern hemisphere, being vaguely Indonesian and vaguely mulatto. But when somebody cradled Susie with any comprehension, she did what Penny did; she got a deep grip on his head of hair with both hands, so that if he bit her he would be scalped—or lose his ears, if he was bald.

A steer named Bar-B-Que was raffled under a quarter moon. Wednesday had been perfect weather; on Thursday high humidity and a hot sun cut attendance until sundown; the third day was a dry scorcher; the fourth day there were showers; and by the fifth day, Sunday, people were tired, though the weather cleared and cooled. A livestock cavalcade, another display of the march from birth to death, was held; also a parade of milk coolers and snowmobiles. The trotting horses raced, their gait oddly manlike, an unnatural-looking, pumping step corresponding to heel-and-toe. It made them seem six-legged, crablike, although their bodies still gracefully waved like satin ribbons around the track. But I was only raggedly interested in these events by now. Caressing women loosens and softens us for caressing children later on or it's soon wearisome, as in a girlie show, and lately I was thinking that even the supposedly Bedouin austerity of being alone in crowds might not be strengthening or Bedouin at all—merely lonesome—maybe I was getting old.

I talked with Nancy and Leigh Heisinger, the Sensational Leighs. He's a practical, physical young man from

Tallahassee, and his wife is timidly pretty, especially in costume, with girlish pigtails—not really a show person, more like a child bride. He has a fluty voice and struck me as light-headed and rather dumb, but he does "walk in space," romping in the air, a spinning, running, rhythmic spectacle, as much as fifty feet high. The Loop Swing, as he calls it, is like two blades of a windmill, each end having a hoop attached where Heisinger and his wife walk as the blades turn so that they balance one another and regulate the rotations, propelling themselves. She's not as good, and when he hangs a weight on the opposing spoke and performs on his own, he rollicks in the air, with music in his motions, outdoing himself.

Mrs. Smoky Gilmore looks like a woman in a comic strip: the widow woman down the block who cuts an eccentric figure, stomping around, good-humoredly muttering to herself. She wears mud boots and baggy pants and has hair like tarred, unraveled rope, but she's her husband's partner; she works in a centrally located peanut booth where she can watch the action and what's going on and who is who. Smoky stays in their trailer, available for consultation. He sits near the doorway, leaning heavily on his elbows. He is an unshaven Irishy man of middle age with a great stomach but sturdy legs. He has a year-round lumbering business in Maine and runs the carnival from May to October. The logging is a better life but the carnival is "a challenge among men," he says —other men are always trying to take it away from him or pinch his profit margin. "You're either cut out for it or you're not." I made several attempts to see him before he was free. Either he would have a visitor or he'd be on the telephone to Seattle for a replacement part or would be "wrapping money" with his back to me—"Gotta lot of money to wrap." It's not as rough a business now in terms of whom you hire (many a mother's pretty son is going native just for the summer), but getting any help at all is harder; he must quintuple the old salaries. Also, to take an example, he paid $10,000 in rent to set up at the Lobster Festival in Rockland, Maine, for a skimpy three days, and one day's rain hurt him badly. He has fourteen county fairs to play this year, but although everybody wants a carnival for old time's sake, they want it to be extra clean—no "controlled" joints, "bucket" joints or "swing" joints, where the operator decides who wins, and which, along with the rides, should be the backbone of a carnival's profits. "There's only so many dart-balloons and duck-ponds that you can put in."

Smoky started with a balloon joint thirty years ago and gradually amassed a show. Just in the minutes I was with him, a woman customer came to report that the Ferris-wheel driver was drunk (untrue) and that the cotter on one of the seats had wiggled loose and two kids had almost fallen out. Then Penny, the mama from the French Quarter, ran up with her big barker to report a fight; a troublemaker had hit them both. A detective appeared too. And Mr. Conley stopped by, asking for Smoky's check for the week's rent. Smoky didn't want to pay it yet in case he needed bargaining power later on. Smiling, he said his wife had to co-sign and that she was busy on the Midway. Conley, lanky-looking, was stumped. He seemed uneasy at my presence too, as if afraid I might be going to pillory him the way he thought the *Life* reporter had done. Smoky chatted away indicating that I was welcome to stay as long as Conley did. In fact, though, it was during these interludes when Conley was trying to deal with the show-business folk that I liked him best. He was outclassed and kind of a hillbilly, and yet he seemed more tolerant of them than some of the other local men. His pride at the fair's whirlyburl was likable, but then you'd see him over in the parking lot with a bunch of tough young country boys, a snicker on his mouth.

On the last night the broad grounds were illuminated with islets of light; a band played high-pitched hectoring music, the trombones fluff-fluff-fluffing underneath. The Cyclonians practiced their lifts; they were off to Sherbrooke, Quebec, the next day. The vendors caught the excitement of winding up: "Hamburgers with stinky onions! Hamburgers with stinky onions!" "*Roll it, roll it, roll it!*" the Ringling Bros. straw bosses used to yell on nights when there was a teardown. Everybody's worth was measured by how fast he did his job. Now each individual package of a stage show packs up separately, some waiting till the morning to leave, others, like Happy Davis, who is impatient, pulling away immediately.

Guy Gossing's tigers, lying in their row of boxes thirstily, watched Gossing's German shepherd drink. He watered them and limped about barefoot, doing housekeeping chores. He was sweating and drinking Pepsi after the vicissitudes of the last performance. His father owned a circus in Europe, and now he has to drive himself between obscure fairgrounds. Speaking a weighty, accented, staccato speech, sniffing because of the pain that his broken hand caused him, he said it was easier for the animals than for him. He said he'd worked with leopards, whose small faces are difficult to read, but had come to America with a cheery gang of lions, then sold them and bought these tigers. Mrs. Gossing was sneezing from the Vermont combination of cold midnights and August days. The tigers, filling up their boxes—huge painted-pasteboard faces—had galvanized themselves, with Gossing's help, into a headlong sendoff show, as if to make this exit memorable. Gossing had jerked and jumped in the essential gestures like an old boxer, conveying a sense, above all, of the labor involved in earning a living. After dismantling the act cage and cleaning up, he finished watering Rajah, who was the biggest, and touched noses with him.

I too used to finish my work at night by giving water to a tiger called Rajah and touching noses with him (how many tigers have performed under that stilted name?), so I felt nostalgic, driving away. I was relieved that the week of crowds was over and that the next month would be a quiet one for me. But I still love crowds, just as I still love tigers, and keep going back at convenient occasions to feel the breath of each: neither taste withers away with age. Since we're all brothers to the tiger, we will probably find some kind of substitute for him when he's extinct. And since we're all mob-lovers as well as Bedouins, we will continue to mix delight and despair equally, churning in churning crowds.

HOME
IS TWO
PLACES

Things are worse than many of us are admitting. I'm a brassbound optimist by habit— I'm an optimist in the same way that I am right-handed, and will always be. It's simpler to be an optimist and it's a sensible defense against the uncertainties and abysses which otherwise confront us prematurely—we can die a dozen deaths and then usually we find that the outcome is not one we predicted, neither so "bad" nor so "good," but one we hadn't taken into consideration. In an election, though, for instance, where it's only a question of No. 1 or No. 2, I confidently assume that whoever seems to be the better fellow is going to win. When sometimes he doesn't, I begin to feel quite sure that perhaps the other man, now in a position of responsibility, will shift around to views much closer to my own. If this doesn't occur either, then I fall back on my fuzzy but rooted belief that people of opposed opinions at least do share the quality of good-heartedness, of wanting good things to happen, and so events finally will work out for the best.

The trouble is that they're not working out for the best. Even the cheerfully inveterate sardonicists, whose chirpy pessimism is an affirmation of sorts, are growing dispirited and alarmed. And it's not just the liberals; the unease emanates from everybody, Republicans and Christian Scientists—the lapel buttons and bumper stickers and decal figures imply a kind of general clamming-up, a sense of being beleaguered, maybe a panic at the great numbers of people we each pass in a single day—this with the hardening of sects of opinion which have despaired of conversing with one another but only holler out code words and threats. Many people think about finding some peaceful holing-up spot, which may be in the suburbs, or if the individual has already opted for the suburbs, may be up toward Mount Katahdin. As soon as he can afford it he starts wanting a second home, a place to recuperate from the place where he lives while he works, and though it used to be that such a home was frankly a luxury, now nearly everybody who makes a middle-class living starts to think about buying a cottage in the woods or a boat at the shore, if just for the sake of his health. The thirty-hour week, so heralded, may mean three hard ten-hour days of work in the city and then a fast retreat for everybody (in shifts) to what will pass for "the country" in twenty years, there to lead the leisure life, building canoes and greenhouses and picket fences.

I grew up in the suburbs. My father left for New York City every weekday morning and got home about 7 P.M. The commuting was grueling and he liked a change of

scene on his vacations in later years, but we didn't need
to have a country cottage, since we saw deer in the evening and grew a Victory Garden during the war; there
was a feed store in town, painted with checkerboards,
where the local farmers talked about chicken diseases
and trapping weasels. A man named Frank Weed trained
pheasant dogs professionally, and my sister when she was
growing up went across the road and watched a calf born
every spring. Both she and I spent part of our childhoods
developing a special sympathy for the animal personality.
There was a magical fullness to my perceptions when I
was with my dogs, a heat-lightning shiver and speed,
quicker than words. Of course to rule is a pleasure, and
yet as happiness, as intimacy, these interludes are not to
be dismissed, and the experience of sensing other wave
lengths in the world besides the human gabble needs
woods and fields and isn't found as easily now.

The out-of-doors was everything to me. I spent the
summer mornings on Miss Walker's big estate, vaulting
the brooks, climbing the pines, creeping along the rabbit
paths. Then I made lemonade for the afternoon heat wave
and lay on the screen porch listening to Mel Allen broadcast the Yankee game. There'd be a thunderstorm and I
would lie in the backyard for that, watching the black
clouds brew, feeling the wind. Soaked, grinning, I'd go
and sit inside the chicken coop for the clubbiness of the
chickens, whose pecking order I knew all about. Later I
traveled to prep school carrying my alligators wrapped in
a blanket to protect them from the cold. But I loved
Tommy Henrich too; I was a hero-worshiper. And at

night, when I was jittery, I returned to the city, where I'd lived earlier; in the most frequent dream I jumped off the Empire State Building and flew with uneven success between the skyscrapers by flapping my arms. Winters were spent in galoshes, fooling on the schoolbus. Those bus rides were the best part of the day; we had no teacher accompanying us and the driver put up with anything. There was a boy who kept a Model A to tinker with when he got home; another was the quarterback who won our football games; another the school mathematician or "brain." The mechanic has since turned into a clergyman, the quarterback works humbly for General Electric, the mathematician is mad. One nondescript goof-off has made a million dollars, and his chum of the period is a social worker with addicts. Of my own friends, the precocious radical has become a stockbroker and the knockabout juvenile delinquent journeys now in Africa. The same sea changes seem to have affected even the houses that I knew. Mrs. Holcomb's, where I took piano lessons, is now the Red Cross Headquarters; Dr. Ludlow's, where I went for inoculations, has become the town museum. Miss Walker's woodsy acres are the Nature Study Center, and the farm where my sister watched the calves born—Mr. Hulendorf's—has been subdivided into a deluxe set of hutches called Historic Homes.

Wherever, whoever we were, we've been squeezed out of the haunts of our childhood, and there is no reason why we shouldn't have been. The question is only whether we are gradually being squeezed out of all possible homes. To the fear of dying of the ailments that killed our fathers, of angina or driving badly, we have an added, overlying trepidation that life may be shortened anyway for all of us. Old age seems not to exist as a possibility culturally, in any case, and the generalized future seems incomprehensible—exploding, crazily variant developments to be fitted together. The more successful and propulsive a man of affairs is, the more freckled and browned he usually looks, so that when he finally folds up in exhaustion, he must correspond to a tree which has turned to punk inside the bark invisibly and which suddenly crumbles. Aging used to be a slow process involving wasting less and less of one's energy as well as having less energy, and so, for a long while at least, the pleasure in one's increased effectiveness just about balanced the sadness of winding down. And as a man lost some of his youthful idealism, he lost, too, some of the brutality that goes along with being young: a balance was maintained there also. Now he's either young or on the shelf, and if he's on the shelf he's savage.

When my father was dying I had a dream which amounts to a first memory, brought up intact like some frozen fossil which the ice has preserved. I was diapered, lying on my back in his hands, well before I could talk. By comparing my size in his hands to my daughter's right now I would guess that I was about ten months old. I was struggling, kicking, and he was dandling me, blowing in my ear, a sensation too ticklish, too delicious to bear. Squealing, powerless to prevent his doing it, I loved it, though at the same time I was dependent upon him to stop before it became excruciating—I was waving my arms in the air trying to protect my ears. But the best, vividest piece of the memory is the whirring, vital presence of my father, with deep eyes and a humming voice, in the prime of life; I remember his strong hands. Even his early baldness seemed to add to his vigor because it made for more area of skin. He was several years younger than I am now, and so the continuity of seeing him then and myself now, and seeing him die, is startling.

This memory feeds on to the pinpoint events of a train wreck in Nebraska a year later, and to the familiar jumble of childhood. During the Depression we lived in the city; there were singers at the bottom of the air shaft whom the maid and I threw dimes down to, wrapped in toilet paper so that they wouldn't bounce too far. I pulled the bow of her apron to tease her twenty times a day, and she took me to Catholic church, whose mysteries I remember better than the inside of our church, though once recently when I was hurrying along Lexington Avenue I was brought up short by the sight of a mnemonic worn brick wall that shook me: Sunday School. My parents reappeared in youthful roles, and I could remember something about that whole extraordinary masquerade which one plays as a child—pretending to learn to read, as if we didn't know already, pretending to learn to tell the time, as if we hadn't known all about clocks for years and years.

My father was a financial lawyer. At first I went to an English-type school called St. Bernard's and to birthday parties at the St. Regis Hotel. I remember, too, watching King George pass in a cavalcade on Fifth Avenue from a dowager's wide windows. But Eisenhower, another war-time eminence whom I saw feted from those windows, represents much better my father's style. The side of Eisenhower that wasn't glamorous like Clark Gable re-sembled my father—the grin, the Kansas accent, the Middlewestern forehead, the level-headed calmness or caution, the sanguine and good-tempered informality. Each was a poor-boy democrat and a Republican; each stood out for rural, old-time values, though personally preferring to hang out at the golf club with industrialists; each was softer in manner than the average soldier or lawyer; and each had a Chinese face lurking behind the prosaic American bones which materialized inchmeal as he aged and died. My father worked in Eisenhower's administration, and Ike was the president he most ap-proved of—an internationalist abroad, a gentle-minded conservative on the home front, who started, however, from the assumption that most people deserved to be liked.

Once when my father was leaving a Mario Lanza movie he stopped to hear one last aria again, and collapsed with emotion on the floor of the theater when it ended. And, if he hadn't much sense of humor (or it came hard to him), he laughed a lot, loudly, every chance he had. He thought that exercise, music and friends were the cure for mental illness: in other words, it terrified him. He thought homosexuality "sinister" on the occasions when he recognized it, and never drank much, and probably was sexually faithful, although I think he fooled himself about the nature of certain avuncular relationships he had; when one young woman married he tore her honeymoon picture in half. But his marriage wasn't unhappy. Quite often he ended his friendships with men who got divorced on what he considered frivolous grounds; he didn't swear or like swearing, although he liked vitality and a masculine air in his friends. He had the chest of a track man and may have read more passionately as a man of sixty than as a college boy, which is unusual—he was especially partial to translated classics and to looking at Renaissance art. Mother married him partly because of his idealism, she says, though naturally I didn't think him idealistic at all. I even went to a different barber in town as a means of delineating the difference between us. Mine was the Town Barbershop, which had *Liberty* magazine beside the chairs and a proprietor nearly eighty years old, wonderfully wiry and tall, with black hair, knotted hands and a sharp nose. For the many years I went to him he knew me as "Peter"—in the beginning I'd been too shy to set him straight. The Colonial Barbershop, which my father patronized, did a smoother job, and the owner, who was a worldly man, tried at one point to break out into the wholesale barbering-supply business but went bankrupt and soon was right back in the local shop. After that, he spent his weekends in New York, wandering reflectively among the skyscrapers, musing on the enigmas of fortune and wealth.

My father was battling for advancement at the same time, trying to rise from the position of a hired attorney to a directorship in the oil corporation he worked for. He wasn't an original type or a sparkplug—he seemed awfully meticulous—and so he lost. He went into retirement angry, though several offers came his way thereafter, such as to go to Hong Kong as consul or head a graduate school. Instead he drifted, wrote poetry and went to Kyoto. When the World's Fair played on Long Island he drove out and roamed the cheerful pavilions, scanning the Midwestern faces, delighted by the accents, reminded of his boyhood; like the Fair itself, he was hopeful. In manner, he was so deliberate some of the other commuters had called him Speed, and yet late in his life he traveled round the world, pulling my mother after him when her enthusiasm waned. He returned to Rome and Paris ten or twelve times, and he loved Florence—nothing that a thousand other men don't do but with as much intensity as any. Dutch Reform by background, he shifted towards agnosticism in middle age, joining the Episcopal Church as a form of neutralism. He liked to sail, sailed rather daringly, not with the caution that exasperated some business associates. He sent money to relatives who had hard rows to hoe and liked uninfluential people as well as the strong. For instance, when I was a boy he made me aware of a fellow at the oil company whose function was to meet transatlantic ships and speed the debarking of company bigwigs and guests—a tall, prudent, intelligent-looking man of mature years whom one would see standing among the crowd of passengers' relatives and friends as the ship docked. Noticeable for his banker's dress and for his height, he would step forward through the multitude and fix upon the personage he was supposed to meet (I suppose he studied photographs), bring over a Customs man, somehow accelerate the inspection, get porters, flag down a taxi, and see the mogul whisked away before most of the passengers were even off the boat. My father was touched by his plight.

When it was possible to procrastinate, my father did so, being a dreamy man, but he was decisive at the end. He went for a sail alone overnight in his little sloop before turning himself in, exhausted, to the doctor, with cancer signals, and while he was waiting to die, still ambulatory, he journeyed to Sarasota with my mother. She could scarcely get him to leave before it was too late for him to go under his own power, but then he settled into the house in Connecticut for the last siege with gallantry and gaiety, so that the big busty nurse, accustomed though she was to seeing men die, actually fell in love with him and became inconsolable. He enjoyed the ripening spring weather, the phonograph, the house he loved, and kept hold of his self-command (what, after all, can one do with one's time in those last weeks except to be friendly?). He talked on the telephone, blinked in the brightening sun—to overhear him in the final conversations he had with friends was piercing. And he did want the Church to fulfill its appointed duties, so when a cub minister was sent to visit him he wasn't satisfied with the small talk they were able to muster. Then an old senior minister, a tippler with a crumpled face, came and told him that he faced "a great adventure," which he accepted as being probably about as good a construction as anybody was going to be able to put on it. My mother saw horses with blowing manes climbing the sky for weeks after he died.

If we are to contrive to lead two lives now, one in the city and one near Katahdin, we can draw some quick assurance from the fact that our backgrounds individually are even more diverse than that. I've got millers, tailors and outdoorsmen in mine, real outdoorsmen to whom the summer soldiers' Katahdin would be a tasty canapé. Though the two names, Morley and Hoagland, fit together neatly for me because I'm so used to them, the families—my mother's and father's—stretch back in complicated, quite disparate fashion, the Hoaglands to early Brooklyn; later they lived in New Jersey. They came out badly in the Revolutionary War—the branch of them I know about. A skirmish with the British a few minutes' walk from their farm put several of them out of commission for the rest of their lives. The ones who weren't too demoralized moved west and south shortly afterwards to Lexington, Kentucky, where they did fairly well, except that again my own ancestors after a generation or so migrated on by boat and wagon to the farming country of Bardolph, Illinois, where they spent the Civil War. One who had marched with Sherman creaked on from Bardolph by wagon to Hutchinson, Kansas, where he farmed a Soldier's Land Claim, kept a hotel, and worked with team and wagon on the construction of the Santa Fe, and wound up as the county agricultural agent and a Freemason. Though there were proud Eastern Hoag-

lands who belonged to the upper crust, and other Hoaglands who split away to seek lonelier, unknown destinies,
most of my branch of the family were farmers consistently
for two or three hundred years, right back to Brooklyn,
and they appear to have filtered away into the soil finally,
or else to have wound up in Los Angeles with the rest of
the prairie farmers who scraped together a few thousand
dollars, there joining the middling middle class.

One early pale fellow loyally fought cholera in the
Kentucky epidemic of 1823, dying at his post, and my
grandfather, who was a doctor too, died abruptly of
meningitis in the 1930s after a bumpy career, mostly prac-
ticing obstetrics in Kansas City. He was a husky-faced,
square-set man with a red complexion, certainly a kindly
doctor, but he found it hard to make a living and for
several interludes went down to the bayou lumber camps
in Louisiana to work as a company physician. His oldest
child died of a fever on one of these tours of duty; his
youngest died in his arms after being hit by a trolley a
little bit later. His wife, too, died young. I have the impression that his happiest years were while he was in the
Medical Corps during the First World War. He and my
father got along quite well, and my father, despite his
successes and travels later on, would have gone to the state
university and presumably stayed in Kansas City if at
the last minute he hadn't noticed a scholarship competition for Yale on his school's bulletin board. Being a lawyer
and the son of a doctor, he thought of us as a family of
professionals and hoped that I would enter one of the
professions—if not either of those, then what he called

"the cloth"—rather than be a businessman. When I wound up a writer he was utterly taken by surprise.

The Morleys, by contrast, were merchants instead of farmers for as far back as I am aware. They arrived in the New World after the Hoaglands did, and whatever matters they applied themselves to when they first got off the boat, they were in upstate New York for a while before settling in Painesville, Ohio, in the nineteenth century. The Morley burial plot is still in Painesville, along with a rambling white house with long porches and a poppy and gentian field in the rear—a sort of family "seat," which the Hoaglands lack. It was partly the Morleys' clannishness that put me off them when I was a boy. By 1900 they were worthy people with fat family businesses, big family weddings—the marriages were patriarchal; none of your warlike American ladies there— and they kept right on flourishing, until by the time Franklin D. Roosevelt campaigned through town, some of them wouldn't even walk down to the railroad depot just to set eyes on the man. Since I'd been brought up among the comforts my father's breadwinning had earned, these shrewd breadwinning businessmen from Painesville, and Saginaw, Michigan, and Aberdeen, Washington, seemed like vaguely unsavory bores to me. The family dinners, occurring whenever there was a visit, intimidated me; the questioning was bluff, immediate and intimate, as if blood were thicker than water. Yet I remember that when my Great-uncle Ralph came east for the last time, knowing he was soon to die, he rented his suite at the Biltmore, invited my father up, and spent that last interview with us reading aloud with relish the notebook notations he kept in an inside pocket of what his stock-market portfolio was. My father, who had nothing to do with handling the Morleys' money, was astonished. This stingy or mercenary quality afflicting many of the Morleys is in me also, but they were a florid, varied crew whom a less Protestant person than myself would have found fascinating from the start, and next to whom we of the present tribe are insipid fellows. The Morleys are following the Hoaglands into modest extinction, part of the Johnny Carson family.

My mother's family's pride and principal vocation during the time between the two world wars was Morley Bros., a department store and statewide hardware dealership located in Saginaw. Before opening that, her grandfather had had a saddlery business in Chicago, after leaving Painesville as a young man. While getting his Chicago operation going, he married a packinghouse heiress, a Kelley (the family had sold out to Armour). Later, in Saginaw, he founded a bank as a kind of a sideline. Banking intrigued him, but during the 1929 boom he sold the bank to a big Detroit bank that was looking for mergers. He happened to be in New York City on a business trip in October during the first black days of the Crash. Realizing the seriousness of the situation, realizing that the Detroit bank was over-committed and might have to close, he hated to think of his own town's bank collapsing along with it, and so he caught a Pullman home. The panic was spreading west, the officers in Detroit already saw the handwriting on the wall, and hurrying to rally the help of a few other Saginaw citizens, he was able to buy back the bank and save it, in a fine hour. Banks were still a centerpiece in the post-Victorian era and banks do figure on this side of my family; this same ancestor's daughter-in-law, my grandmother, had grown up in Homer, New York, the child of the local bank president. But they'd had to sneak out of town in sudden disgrace during the 1893 Panic when their bank failed. Her father's health foundered in the aftermath; he died, and she weathered some very hard years.

At any rate, Morley Bros. prospered. My great-grandfather toured the world with his beautiful chestnut-haired Kelley, leaving Ralph in charge of the Saginaw business and A. J., my grandfather, based in Chicago running the older saddlery firm. There were two other brothers, Walter and Paul. Paul was a Peter Pan type who loved combing my mother's hair when she was a young girl (it was the Kelley hair). An esthete and idealist, he hobnobbed with landscape painters and portrait artists and married a girl of nineteen who was so very demure and Alice-like that she proved to be feeble-minded. He died at only forty-six, welcoming death, so it is said, and leaving behind five blighted children who suffered from St. Vitus dance, and worse. Walter, a more earthly man, was a gambler and womanizer, a failed writer and, later in life, a Presbyterian minister, who lived in relative poverty, exiled by his father to the Wisconsin woods after some early miscues. However, Walter was the first of the Morleys to venture out to the state of Washington. He got mixed up in some kind of woman scandal and went badly into debt to the sawmill promoters of Aberdeen, and A. J. was sent west to buy them off. After Walter had been extricated, though, A. J. went to work investing in timber himself. Bored with Chicago saddlery, he became a pioneer businessman in the Gray's Harbor woods. When his first wife died in childbirth, he married my grandmother, whom he met in a tiny town where she was schoolteaching and where he'd missed his train. Soon he had three trains of his own for hauling logs, and a house on the hill, a yacht, a mistress in downtown Aberdeen (also a schoolmarm, oddly enough), a burro for his children, and a manservant, Tom. Land that he bought for $7000 and logged was sold recently for $3,000,000. He was a careful, decent man with no archenemies, although he fought the Wobblies, and he and Ralph had pleasing sons. Both he and Ralph partook of the Morleys' honest but griping conservatism about money, which ultimately prevented them from getting big-time. Back in Michigan, Ralph turned down a neighbor named Henry Ford who wanted him to invest in a motorcar company, while out in Aberdeen a decade or two later A. J. declined the chance to buy a new corporation called Boeing. His eldest boy had been killed by a falling tree, but he and his other two sons put their resources into timberland in the Oregon Coast Range instead. One was a financial man, at ease with the business community in Portland; the other, silver-haired before his mid-thirties, could deal with the loggers and union men and drove around through the mountains all day in his pickup truck. Unfortunately, the financial son dropped dead in church in his early fifties. Immediately the hard-nosed investors in Saginaw got scared that my silver-haired uncle would not be able to manage the business alone, and they made him sell out. He did enlist the ladies in the family, who were also stockholders, to help him stave them off when it came to a vote until he'd delayed long enough to get the proper price.

There is much to the Morleys that I don't know about and much to be said for them. Two women of Northern persuasion wrote action-filled, observant diaries during the Civil War, for instance—all about guerrillas and the battlefronts along the Mississippi. But for a long time, certainly throughout my teens, it was my wish to start from scratch and make my own way in the world without the help of relatives. The Morleys were always boosting each other, some were slightly-Babbitt-like, and they assumed, aggravatingly, that any relative was fair game for their gregariousness. Besides, my socialist sentiments leaned more toward the Hoaglands on their dirt farms— they were pleasingly faceless to me, the few I'd seen having just been the Los Angeles transplants. Of course I'd traveled through enough Kansas farming communities to know how little tolerance people there would show for an oddball like me if they perceived my true colors, so, glad to let them remain faceless, I simply liked to think of myself as anchored—in theory, at least—in the heartland, in the Wheat Belt.

Lately it's become the rage to ridicule young radicals from middle-class backgrounds who pretend to themselves that they are black or are blue-collar, when actually all they need to do if things get tough is reach a telephone to raise bail money or be invited home. The ridicule has

been a political weapon because what most bothers
people about these young persons is their accomplishment
in challenging the nation's stance. I was in their shoes in
the 1950s, and we weren't challenging anybody success-
fully; we kept our heads down, lived privately, and we
were few and far between; perhaps the troubles of the
present time may owe a little something to our ineffectu-
ality. But like these activists, I'm sure, I was aware of the
inconsistencies in my own position—being only too eager
to give my parents' suburban address to officialdom if I
edged into a jam instead of my grubby Lower East Side
street number. Despite the inconsistencies, it seemed to
me then that I had the choice of either going out in the
world and seeing what was foreign and maybe wretched,
having experiences which were not strictly necessary in
my case, and *caring*, however uselessly, or else of spending my summer on the tennis courts and terrace at the
country club, as some of my schoolmates were doing. The
head start they supposed they had on people born into
different surroundings has often proved illusory, and anyway the effort to make a beginning on independent lines,
not piggyback on one's father's achievements, seemed admirable, even traditional, in America until recently. It's
just lately, with the exasperated warfare between the
generations, that attempting to make a new start for oneself is ridiculed.

Apart from the fuss of being political, the reasons why
I was so agitated as a youngster, so angry at my parents

that it amounted to a fury lasting for weeks on end, are
difficult to reconstruct; I was a bunch of nerves. My
mother, who besides being impulsive and generous was a
strangely warm woman at times, would ask me to eat
dinner without my glasses on so she could look at my
uncluttered face, and tried to insist that I move down
from the third floor to the room next to hers. Sometimes
after my father and I had had a conciliatory talk, she'd
give me a quite opposite report of what he thought, or
thought of me, as though to revive the quarrel. Later, in
my twenties, looking back, my chief complaint against
him was that he hadn't shielded me from some of her
eccentric whims and decisions; yet I'd fought with him
rather than her, especially when I was in earnest. She
was my cohort, guiding me most directly, and now, when
I put first things first and respond quickly to the moment,
it's her influence. What I learned from him was not the
Boerlike sobriety and self-denial he espoused but the
qualities that I saw for myself: his gentleness and slow-
tempoed soft gaiety, his equanimity under pressure. I
liked the way he ate too; he ate like a gourmet whenever
he could.

Although I would have been willing to ignore most
facets of the life of the town where I grew up, luckily it
wasn't possible for me to do that. So I have the many
loose-leaf memories a hometown is supposed to provide—
of the Kane children, whose father was a gardener and
who threw jackknives at trees whenever they were mad,
which, living as they did in other people's garages, was a
good deal of the time; of setter field trials and local foot-

ball; of woebegone neighbors and abrupt marital puzzles
—a wife who rejoiced when her husband died and buried
him before his friends knew there was going to be a
funeral. There were some advertising people so rich that
they lived in one large house by themselves and kept their
children in another a hundred yards away. There was a
young architect struck into stone with polio, and a lady
who collected impoverished nobles in Italy after the war
and whose husband, left sick at home, made the maid
disrobe at gunpoint when he finally got lonely. On the
dark roads after supper you'd see more than one com-
muter taking a determined-looking constitutional, walking fast for miles, as if to get his emotions under control.

After my father's death we sold our house and set about
looking for new places to consider home, not an easy task.
The memory was of twenty rooms, artesian water, a shady
lawn, a little orchard and many majestic maples and
spruce, all situated where an old crossroads stagecoach
inn had stood. None of us came up with an arrangement
to equal that, but my mother has an apartment in the city
and a trim pretty house on Martha's Vineyard. My
sister married and, with her husband, found a farmhouse
in Connecticut near his work with five or six acres on
which she put ten horses, in order to start a riding stable.
These were snake-necked, branded horses that they'd
brought in a van from California, right off the range, with
a long winter's growth of hair. The neighbors, who believed that life ought to have a dual, contemporary character, rushed to the zoning board to express dismay that
in a fast-developing, year-round community the regula-

tions hadn't yet been revised to bar such activities, which seemed more appropriate to a *summer* home. They were right to think it surprising, and yet the board was awfully reluctant to declare once and for all, officially, that the era of farms and barns had ended. A compromise was struck.

I married too and live in western Greenwich Village, which is an ungeometric district of architecture in a smorgasbord and little stores. There is a massive wholesale meat market in the neighborhood, a gypsy moving industry, many printing plants and bakeries, a trading center for antiques, a dozen ocean-oriented wharves, and four or five hundred mysterious-looking enterprises in lofts, each of which could either be a cover for the Federal Narcotics Bureau or house an inventor-at-work. I like the variety (the mounted police have a stable two blocks away, the spice industry's warehouses are not far south) —I like the low nineteenth-century houses alongside bars with rock jukeboxes and all the swoosh of à la mode. The pull or the necessity of living in the city seems only to grow stronger as every sort of development is telescoped into a briefer span of time. We can either live in our own period or decline to, and to decline revokes many other choices we have. Mostly what we try to do is live with one foot in the seventies and one foot in an earlier decade— the foot that doesn't mind going to sleep and maybe missing something.

I've just bought a house of my own in Vermont, eight rooms with a steel roof, all painted a witching green. It's two miles from the nearest light pole and it was cheap, but it's got forty acres, extending in a diamond shape, that back up to 5000 acres of state-owned land, and stands in a basin just underneath the western-style peak of a stiff little mountain, Wheeler Mountain, that curves around in front. The Wheelers, our only neighbors, live next door on a 300-acre farm, growing up in aspen, balsam, birch and pine, just as our land is. Mr. Wheeler, in his eighties now, was a fireman on the Grand Trunk Railroad for much of his life but grew up here and returned during the Depression. His father had pioneered the land; the Butterfields pioneered mine. The Butterfields built a log house close to that of old Mr. Wheeler, for whom Mr. Butterfield worked. There was a sawmill, a sugar house and even a granite quarry on Wheeler's place. The log house was really more like a root house than living quarters, to judge from the photograph we have, so in 1900 Mr. Butterfield and his three sons built this new home out of sawn spruce and big granite foundation blocks and plaster mixed from sand from the Boiling Spring over the hill. Their lame old horse did the hauling and pulled the scoop when they dug out the cellar hole, and young Wheeler, a schoolboy then, helped nail the laths.

Butterfield was a rough character, he says, "part Indian," as the phrase goes, but you could depend on him to do a job. His mother-in-law lived with the family, constantly fighting with him. She called him dumb and crude because he couldn't do sums, for instance; she wrote a column of numbers on the wall and watched him fail to add it. About 1909 he shot her, took his remaining relatives next door for refuge, and shot himself. There are bullet holes, stopped up with putty, and it is claimed that that nagging column of numbers on the parlor wall had finally been added correctly. Newspaper reporters buzzed around, the property soon passed to the Stanley family, and Burt Stanley, who was a stonemason, farmed it in his spare time until his death in the 1930s. Then a tax bill of $13 came due. His widow, Della, was unable to pay it (some say she paid it but got no receipt), so the town tax collector, a fellow named Byron Bundy, foreclosed and sold her home to a crony of his named Gray, who quickly reconveyed the place to Bundy himself. Bundy died, the house stood empty through World War II (the porcupines chewing away like carpenters at the corners and edges), and his heirs sold it to our predecessors at a joke of a price.

So I'm getting a grip on the ground, in other words— gathering the stories of what went on and poking in the woods. It's certainly not an onerous chore; I've explored so many wood lots which *weren't* mine. Up among the mountain ledges is a cave as big as a band concert shell, and a narrow unexpected swamp with pitcher plants growing in it, very lush, a spring that springs out of a rock, and a huge ash sheltered in a hollow which has disguised its height and kept the loggers and the lightning off. Not far away is a whetstone ledge where a little businesslike mining used to be done. And there are ravens, bats, barred owls, a hawk or two, phoebes under the eaves, and tales of big bears in the pasture and somebody being cornered by a bull. Delphiniums, mint, lemon lilies, catnip, wild roses and marigolds grow next to the house. Storer's snakes live in the woodpile, as well as garter snakes, brick-colored and black. In the spring dogtooth violets come up, and trilliums, Dutchman's-breeches, box-flowers, foamflowers and lady's slippers, and in the fall the fields fill up with goldenrod and brown-eyed Susans, aster, fireweed. Raspberries grow in masses; also black-berries, blueberries, wild cherries and wild plums. The apple orchard is complicated in its plotting, because these farmers wanted apples in late summer—Dutch apples, Yellow Transparents and McIntosh—and then another set of trees which ripened in the autumn, perhaps Bald-wins or Northern Spies, and lastly the hard winter apples, which weren't sweet and which they canned or cooked as applesauce or "sulphured" to keep till spring. An orchard was a man's bequest to his children, being something that they couldn't promptly create for themselves when the land passed to them. I've got more going on on that hill slope of apple trees than I know about, and when the fruit falls finally, the deer and bears eat it—the bears when they have grown impatient waiting have bashed down whole limbs.

In New York my home *is* New York; nothing less than the city itself is worth the abrasion of living there, and the alterations go on so fast that favorite hangouts go by the boards in a month's time; the stream of people and sensation is the thing. But in the country the one word is exactitude. If you don't like the barn behind the house and the slant of the land and the trees that you face, then you're not going to be happy. The Canadian climate of north Vermont makes for an ideal second home because in four months three seasons can be witnessed. June is spring, September already is autumn. The moonlight is wheat-colored in August, and the mountain rises with protean gradualism to a taciturn round peak. On the east face is a wall which, if you walk around that way, can look to be nine thousand feet; the granite turns ice-white. The trees puff in the moonlight to swirling, steeplish shapes, or look like ferns. During the day sometimes a fog will effect the same exaggerated trick. High up, the wind blows harder, gnarling the spruce and bringing clouds swiftly across like those in the high Rockies; you seldom have a sense of just what altitude you're at. Every winter the deer yard under the cliffs in a cedar copse, and on the opposite side, the valley behind the hill that lies behind the Wheelers' house and mine has never been farmed and is so big it is called Big Valley. Vast and thick with trees, it's like an inlet of the sea, sending off a sheen in midsummer as you look down on it.

Mr. Wheeler, the youngest in his family, went to school with the Butterfield children in what is now the Wheelers' house, remodeled and enlarged. He is a broad-shouldered, white-faced man, a machinist at one point, until the dust bothered his lungs. Now he tinkers with his tractor and the power mower, listening to the Red Sox games, although the only professional baseball he ever saw was when he lived in Montreal during the early 1920s. He's a serene, bold man who has survived heart trouble and diabetes and says little but appears full of cheer even when he's angry. Mrs. Wheeler is a dignified, straight-backed woman, quite a reader, and formerly a psychiatric nurse. She once wrote a column for the county newspaper, and used to brew a thousand pounds of cottage cheese during the summer and peddle it among the vacationers, along with strawberries, butter and cream. She keeps a diary and a record of the visitors who come to climb the mountain that we look at, and keeps a calorie count of what her husband eats. She is his second wife, ten years younger. They have a walkie-talkie for communication with the world outside, and extra stocks of food, and a 280-gallon tank of kerosene for heating, so that the snows don't threaten them. The road plugs up but eventually it's plowed; the snow in the fields gets five feet deep and lasts so long "it mosses over—you always get six weeks of March." Being a vigorous walker still, Mrs. Wheeler is even less intimidated than her husband, and in the country style is reticently generous, as realistic as a nurse and farmer's wife combined.

In the old days there was a local man who could run down the deer and knife them, he had such endurance— he could keep up with their first dash, and as they porpoised through the woods, could keep going longer than they could. He hung the meat in a tree by his cabin to freeze, and liked raccoons particularly also, so that by midwinter the tree was strung with upwards of thirty raccoons, skinned and dressed, suspended like white pineapples. Another character, whose complexion was silver-colored, made a regular business out of bountying porcupines. The town paid fifty cents per pair of ears, and sometimes he brought in a hundred pairs. He claimed he had a super-hunting-dog, but actually he was cutting out triangular snips of stomach skin to make a dozen "porcupines" for every one he killed. He didn't do enough real work to break the Sabbath, as they say, and didn't lay in hay enough to last his cattle through the winter, so that by the end of February he would be dragging birch trees to the barn for them to scrape a living from. For spending money, he gave boxing lessons at night in the waiting room of the old railroad station at the foot of the hill. Roy Lord, who lives across from where the station was, learned to box from him. Lord has shot seventy-three deer in his lifetime. He lives with a sneezing parrot fifty-six-years-old, and a bull terrier who lost an eye in a fight in the driveway; he points out the spot where the eye fell. He can recite the details of the murders and suicides in the neighborhood going back forty years—all the fights with fenceposts, all the dirty cheating deals and sudden strange inheritances. He's learned the secrets of more than one suspicious death because he's made it a point over the years to get right to the scene, sometimes even before the police. Or they'd be gathering reinforcements, distributing riot guns and radioing for instructions in front of the house, while Lord would sneak around to the back door and pop inside and see the way the brains were sprayed and where the body lay and where the gun was propped, and damn well *know* it wasn't suicide. There was a family of Indians here, who'd murdered somebody in Canada and buried him in their cellar and moved across the border. They slept on a pile of old buffalo robes laid on the floor. The daughter, a half-breed, went back into the woods in a fit of despondency and found a cliff and jumped. Then when the men had died as well, the last of them, a white-haired old woman, stretched out on the railroad tracks with her neck on a rail and ended it that way. (Lord tells these stories while watching the TV—sheriffs slugging baddies and bouncers punching drunks. His son was a sniper in the Pacific theater, stalking the Japanese like deer; is now a quiet bachelor who works in Massachusetts, driving home weekends.)

I'm transplanting some spruce and beginning to clear my upper field of striped maple and arctic birch. I'm also refashioning a chicken coop to serve as a playhouse when our baby is four or five. The barn is sturdy, moderate-sized, unpainted, built with used planking fifteen years ago. Although the place where I grew up probably had a better barn, I took that one for granted. Now I stand in my own barn and look up at the joists and rafters, the beams under the hayloft, the king posts, struts and studding, the slabs of wood nailed angularly for extra strength. It's all on the same pattern as the other barns in town, and yet I marvel at it. The junk inside consists of whiffle trees, neck yokes and harness, a tractor and a harrow, neither functional, and painters' ladders, milking stools and broken stanchions. In the attic in the house are smaller memorabilia, like fox and beaver traps, deer antlers and tobacco cans of clean deer lard, an old grindstone, an old bedpan, a pair of high green boots, a pile of *Reader's Digests*, which when matched with our assorted miscellany and childhood books, stacked up, and different boxes of letters and snapshots (snapshots of the prairie Hoag-lands seventy years ago, posed in joky insouciance—Hoag-lands who would have felt at home here), will be the attic our daughter grows up to know.

Freight trains hoot through town; there is a busy blacksmith, a Ben Franklin store, and a rest home called Poole's, whose telephone is the night number for all emergency facilities. People say "the forenoon" and say a man whose wife has left him "keeps bachelor's hall." Our predecessors in the house, the Basfords, ate groundhogs parboiled, on occasion, and deer in season and out, and, though we're easier on the game, we cook on their wood stove and light with kerosene, and just as in the platitudes, it's a source of ease and peace. Nothing hokum-yokum, just a sense of competence and self-sufficiency. Every-thing takes time—when it's too dark to read we cook supper, hearing the calling of the owls; then maybe I take the dogs for a walk, playing the part of the blind god. Of course I wouldn't want to get along with wood and kerosene all *winter;* nor do I want to turn the clock back. It's simply doing what is necessary; there is one kind of necessity in the city and another here.

The Basfords only moved around the mountain when we bought their farm. The stove is one Mr. B.'s father bought in 1921—the salesman drove up with a team and wagon piled with iron stoves and told him that if he could break the lid of any of them he could have the whole stove free. The spring we pipe our water from Mr. B. found himself, using water-witching procedures. The first time that he dug a catch-hole he tried enlarging it with dynamite. One stick—detonated with the tractor engine—worked all right, but when he got greedy and wanted still a bigger source, he put in two more sticks and blew the spring away, tipping the base rock so that the water flowed by other routes. He had to go dowsing again, farther from the house, but found a new spot underground where three trickles joined together in front of a tree, and dug more modestly this time, although the overflow was sufficient for Mrs. B. to raise beds of celery there. She's English, once a war bride, now a giggly and seductive woman of about fifty. He is slow-speaking, sharp-witted, rather truculent and rather endearing. He doesn't vote, doesn't get along in town, doesn't work especially hard, doesn't look up to anyone, is an iconoclast. But she admires him. They seem to love each other in absolutely current terms. They're always having coffee, sipping wine, and talking endlessly.

I might as well have begun this essay by saying that things are better than we think. In the public domain they're not, and we can't glance ahead with pleasure to the world our children will inhabit—more than us, perhaps, they will have to swim for dear life. But middle age is the time when we give more than we get—give love, give work, seek sites. And sites can still be found, at least. You may discover you need two houses, but you can find your homes and set to work, living for the decade.